THE

AUTOBIOGRAPHY

OF

MARY SMITH,

SCHOOLMISTRESS AND NONCONFORMIST.

A FRAGMENT OF A LIFE.

WITH

LETTERS FROM JANE WELSH CARLYLE

AND

THOMAS CARLYLE.

LONDON: BEMROSE & SONS.
CARLISLE: THE WORDSWORTH PRESS,
75 SCOTCH STREET.
——
MDCCCXCII.

CHAPTER I.

I was born in an English nonconformist household, of simple country habits, of the order of the common people, without any pretension whatever to wealth or rank, at Cropredy, a village in the north of Oxfordshire, on February 7th, 1822.

My parents, a quite unromantic pair, as it appears, were William Smith, a tradesman, a boot and shoe-maker, a native of that place, and Ann Pride, a Gloucestershire farmer's daughter, who had come thither in the capacity of cook at the vicarage. The Gloucestershire farmers, a hard working thrifty race of people, something like the Scotch, preferred to send their daughters into good service, where they might both learn something and make something, to keeping them at home, and all the more so, when, as was the case in my mother's family, there was a preponderance of girls—more than the household had need of.

My mother had a good deal of ability in her special line—cookery; and hence had travelled about a good deal with the family, a rich pluralist vicar, who had married a duke's daughter. Consequently great style and state were kept up at the vicarage, which was of imposing dimensions; and with its gardens and shrubberies—all closed round with high walls and trees, overtopped and thickly interlaced with ivy—stood in the centre of the village, adjoining the church. The farmers' and tradesmen's houses flanked it all round, while the labouring population lived in poor tumble-down thatched cottages, with dunghills in front of them, at the back of all.

But notwithstanding this, compared with many villages of that period, it was a large, lively, and pleasant one; the Cherwell flowing out of Northamptonshire through its eastern side, and about a stone-throw west of it, on the same side, the Oxford canal, a much more important and busy scene of traffic than at present, both in the coal and carrying trade. All the coal that was then brought from the far north, came by boats by the canal. And in the event of a long frost, when the boats were stopped sometimes for five or six weeks, the coals rose to a great price; the poor at such times being obliged to find their fuel in what they could gather in the fields and woods. On the west of the church —which was a large handsome edifice, and, though apparently many hundred years old, in good repair —ran the highway leading north to Birmingham, and south to London and Oxford, its nearest market being Banbury, a small town, in the centre of an agricultural district, about four miles off, on the Cherwell.

My father was married young, being at the time little more than twenty. My mother was his senior by a year or two. He brought her to his ancestral home, in a row of houses which faced the church. It was built of stone, and thatched, like all the others in the village (except the vicar's); a large rambling house with plenty of room in it; the shop on one side, with its low casement window and half-door, the latter of which hung open all summer long. The dwelling house was on the other side, with its carpetless stone floor and bed rooms and large attics, which last served in after years for additional bed rooms, or store rooms for apples.

My mother was a very industrious, thrifty woman, with a passion for business, though at the time of their marriage, neither of my parents had more than a few pounds beyond their immediate needs. However, her parents made it a rule to give to each daughter on her marriage, fifty pounds, and my mother received this small portion. This probably was the means of setting the young couple forward. At all events, my mother opened a small grocer's shop at the back of the premises. Conjointly, by their industry, they seem to have prospered. I have heard my father say, they saved fifty pounds a year as long as she lived, even with an increasing family around them.

I was the second daughter and fourth child of this union. My mother died of dropsy soon after giving birth to the next child; and the nurse who attended her, became housekeeper to the family. Her death was the beginning of long years of trouble. Strangers and relatives who professed to take an interest in my father's young family, came often for far different ends—to take the furtive opportunity to despoil him of many of mother's treasures. In her travels on the continent, with the vicar's family, she had bought many articles of delft and china of foreign manufacture; also beautiful shawls, crapes, and silks, quite likely to awaken the covetous spirit of unprincipled female relatives.

At last, stimulated possibly by his many difficulties, and his host of false friends, he took the final step of marrying (as many good men have done before,) the housekeeper he had retained from my mother's death, who proved a kind mother to his children, and a very devoted and loving wife to him, through many years of chequered but peaceful life. From this time, the family settled down into something of its old order; though from various reasons, but more especially the loss of my mother's superior business skill, it never quite resumed its former prosperity.

My father, however, had been prepared for these sad events by a great change, which had taken place in his life while my mother yet lived. Like the rest of the tradesmen of the village before that event, he had thought it his first duty to go to church, to please the vicar; but now old things had passed away, and all things had become new. And this great change in his life had strengthened his spirit to bear these trials, and had made him an earnest and loving servant, and a true and fearless disciple of Christ. At another village, called Great Bourton, about a mile off, there was, and still is, a small Independent chapel, which had originally been one of Lady Huntingdon's. A Mr. Hood was stationed at that time at this chapel, and after him a gentleman of the name of Styles, who afterwards rose high in the denomination and became Dr. Styles.

Under the preaching of Mr. Hood, my father—who had previously been a churchman and a worldly man, without any special religious light or knowledge, as were the whole village population, with hardly an exception—became a truly devoted spiritual man and a nonconformist, joining this poor small band of Independents, at Great Bourton. Being now Puritan in life and Calvinistic in creed, all things became new in our house.

One of the first things I discerned in my early childhood was, that my father was not like other men; that he did not swear, nor get drunk, nor indulge in loud, foolish, and filthy conversation, nor did he get into towering passions; but was, at all times, a sober, sensible, gentle, and patient man; and was always ready to do good and assist in any way he could, others who might be in difficulties.

I found early in life, that we were disdainfully called "Meetingers," "dissenters," etc., and regarded as queer folk. Often when a child, as I trotted silently by my father's side down the village street, I saw, as we came to the corners—then the habitual evening lounge of the wickedest and worst of the young men and boys of the parish—coarse jests and rude laughter would precede our arrival, though they generally dropped silent as we passed. But none of these things moved him. He seemed oblivious to all scornful treatment. He had as kindly a smile and as cheery a face and word for the next poor person we met, as though nothing had happened.

My father was a better educated man than almost any of his neighbours. Not that he had been sent to any other school than the one in the village, to which the squire's and rich farmers' children alike went, but he must have been either more studious or else had better abilities. Such men by character and conduct did a great deal towards the enlighten-ment of England. Spoken against on all occasions

—as they were by careless church-going people, and the dissolute of all classes—shrewder observers did not fail to note that they lived more consistent lives, and displayed greater knowledge and thought, than others who filled similar stations in life.

But before passing to speak of other things, I deem it better to try and recollect something of these Nonconformist divines, Mr. Hood and Dr. Styles, who changed the current and character not only of my father's life, but that of many around us. Mr. Hood—whose preaching led to the somewhat rigorous adoption, as it would be now thought, of Puritan piety and practice—was a man, as was Dr. Styles, of a beautiful simplicity of life and conversation and unostentatious piety. In private life, both men were blameless, studying in much opposition and unprovoked abuse, to give offence to no one, however rudely they might be assailed by others. They were men of gentle speech and manners, very unlike the haughty vicar, who walked through the village as the lord and master, and to whom the poor women and girls made their profoundest curtsies, and the poor men and boys their most abject and servile bows.

But the secret of these noiseless evangelizers of England was their earnestness, their deep-rooted enthusiasm and sincerity, which became in time to be felt by their hardest and vilest calumniators. Mr. Hood went from the small chapel at Great Bourton to one near Birmingham; and whoever may have had the good fortune to have heard John Angell James preach at Carr's-lane Chapel, Birmingham, has heard the same style of preacher, and seen the same style of man, only largely magnified. Still there was a great similarity. Their object, end, and spirit being to win the hearts of their hearers; and both alike had that even flow of soft persuasive eloquence so winning in its effects and bearing.

The roughest of the villagers sometimes acted as partisans of the church, and the vicar was known to be intolerant and even violent against any one presuming to teach or preach outside its domain. On one occasion, a young Primitive Methodist had the courage to attempt to preach in the village street. I remember it well, though considerably more than fifty years ago. He came from another village about two miles off. It was a fine moonlight night in winter, and we were aroused from our

family quiet, by an unusual noise as of a violent
crowd.   After pausing to listen, my father rose and
took his hat, walking along the village street to see
what it could be.   As usual, I ran by his side, and
we soon reached the scene of action.   A rather
slender young man, with a beaming countenance,
and an open bible in his hand, was standing under
the hedge by the road; while from the lower part
of the village all the roughest and wickedest rabble
had gathered around him with sticks and stones, and
were using vile language and assuming threatening
attitudes.   Had my father not come up at the
moment he did, it is impossible to say what the
consequences might have been.   He at once took
his stand beside the young man, and in a few words
encouraged him to go on.   My father's calm and
determined manner awed the rude multitude, and
as he persisted in standing by him till all was over,
the rabble subsided into quietness or else slunk
away.

I was very young at the time, but I still remember
how earnestly the young Primitive prayed, kneeling
on the bare ground, that fair moonlight night, my
father standing guard beside him, with the rough

restless crowd seething in front of them. Such scenes as these are now for ever at an end in our villages. Dissent has helped to evangelize the fox-hunting, wine-bibbing vicars almost everywhere; or else ritualism has taught them to furbish up the old church weapons, and interest the people with new and singularly bizarre services.

Fifty years ago, church-going meant little more than keeping on good terms with the vicar, and his obese satellites, the churchwardens, at the small inconvenience of spending a sleepy hour in the high-backed crimson-cushioned pew at the old parish church on a Sunday. Neither Tractarian nor Puseyite had as yet made itself felt; and in town and country alike, one dead dreary level of formality prevailed. No one expected anything new or striking. The vicar's pompous pronunciation of his read discourse, roused no one to listen or to think. The only sentence clearly heard being the final one, "Now to God the Father, God the Son, and God the Holy Ghost," which bit of orthodoxy woke up alike the poor sleepy, hard working, ill-fed, and ignorant village labourer, and the squire and his haughty dame (unobserved in their cosy slumbers) in their high-backed pew.

These, I have often thought, were the earnest and true days of dissent of every name. They were stung into faithfulness by the persecutions of the church. A broad line of unworldliness separated them from their neighbours. The Methodists had already one of their little chapels at Cropredy. A rich miller, more liberal and less prejudiced than most people, had allowed them to build, up a lane behind some property of his. But this little place, notwithstanding its obscure position, prospered and grew amazingly. Truly Methodism has done a blessed work in England. There Sunday after Sunday came men without education, mostly farmers and small tradesmen, sometimes even labourers, from the villages round, who, in spite of their defective school training, had reverent and enthusiastic audiences, and whose unlettered eloquence created the deepest impression on their hearers, and often effected the great change of the " New Birth."

I well remember the earnest style of a good old Methodist farmer, who came occasionally to preach in the little chapel, of whose piety no one had any doubt, though some might smile at his fervid oratory. I can see him now, in my mind's eye, his partially grey scattered locks hanging over his temples, overshadowing soft gray eyes, which were forever changing with his changeful utterances, from the sternest utterances to the most tender looks.

I went regularly, at an early age, to the Methodists' Sunday-school, and received many lasting impressions there. I still remember with gratitude many good men and women who were teachers there, hard workers during the week, but at their post on Sundays, with beaming faces and genial, loving hearts. They knew little of what the world calls learning, but the great spiritual truths of religion had a deep hold of their hearts. I delighted very much in that Sunday-school, and believe it helped to bias my mind for many good impressions.

CHAPTER II.

A CHILD'S education begins early. We might say with its first breath, but certainly long before it goes to school. Left as I was, being only two years old when I lost my mother, I had to amuse myself anywhere, so long as I could be kept out of mischief. Hence I was often in the shop with my father, who had at that time in his employment two brothers, very nice religious men, named Thomas and William Hunt, the former consumptive, a great reader and naturally studious. As a child, I was very fond of this Thomas Hunt. He was very gentle and quiet, for a working man. I remember him telling little amusing rhymes, which always delighted me. On occasions when the shop was clear of customers, my father and he were sure to be busy talking of abstruse matters of theology, or discussing questions of doctrine, or the various "views" of popular preachers whom they had heard.

During these discussions, Thomas would be sitting at his bench and pursuing his work; while my father stood at the cutting board, a long board which hung by hinges, where he usually stood cutting out various kinds of boots and shoes.

As a child of five or six, I was delighted with the quietude of the place, wherein, for instance, I soon learned the difference between man and man, and early felt something of the calm uplifting which these exercises diffused. The sharp beating out of the leather on the lapstone, by no means interfered with the discussion, which still went on, or was taken up again, in the pauses of this cheerful noise, seeming, by the way, to lighten the labour which never for a moment ceased.

I cannot remember the time when I could not read, although I can remember much while very young. I must have been about four years old when I was sent to school. I recollect my father sometimes coming to meet me at twelve o'clock at noon, on a path over the churchyard, and seating me on his shoulder to get a ride; his head bare, and his happy face bright with childish talk to his little "wench." This was a dame's school, kept by an old lady, sister of one of the freeholders of the parish, who lived in a large, rambling, dark, old house, adjoining the churchyard; where the sun rarely came, and where the older boys sometimes caught owls in going home, among the dense masses of ivy with which it was covered. Indeed, so thick was the lane leading by it, that it was commonly called "Hell Hole."

The old dame at the school was a very antique specimen of humanity. She wore an old-fashioned thick muslin cap of Queen Elizabeth's day, the plaited border of which met under the chin. She had a low bodice, wearing a coloured handkerchief under, and sleeves to the elbow, while the half skirt hung bobbed behind, with a blue striped thick woollen Jersey apron, that nearly met around her. Such was the old dame's dress, morning, noon, and night. It seemed to match with her dark house, and with the ample cornered fireplace, by the side of which she always seemed to sit. She had two little forms, which were the sum total of her school furniture; and from these seats she called, one by one, all the little ones to her knee to read. She sometimes pinned them to her knee for punishment, and always wore the same hard look of stern authority.

I never remember to have had any lesson or tuition at all at Dame Garner's school. From a little incident that occurred while I was there, and which I have always remembered distinctly, as the first moral impression I received, I infer that I could even then read well enough to make out the real sense and meaning of an ordinary book. I sat a silent observer on the form by the dark window, sometimes picking up a stray leaf of one of the old torn primers, the only books which the old dame had in her possession. Thus it came about. One afternoon, being in school earlier than the rest, I had got hold of one of these fragments, which had on it a little hymn by Dr. Watts. Simple as these lines are, they seemed to penetrate my very soul, and were never afterwards forgotten.

> When Music's daughters shall go by,
> And you no music hear.

Possibly I sat on the old dame's forms with the rest of the little children for a year or two, but I have an impression that I learnt nothing or next to nothing during that time. She kept all quiet; and

I. 2

did her little household turns before her scholars—setting out her tiny cups and saucers, and her equally tiny teapot, on her three-legged table by the fireside, without cloth or tray. Well do I remember the old dame's brimming cup of black tea—milkless and, probably, sugarless—which she drank before us all, her face as dark as the darkest day in winter. No smile was ever seen to illuminate her stern countenance, from the time of our arrival at school, to the time we made our curtsies and hurried out of it.

Nearly sixty years have passed since I sat in her snug and sunny orchard, a little child among other children, of whom but one or two of many are now left; and yet how real it all seems—my youthful companions and playmates flit before my vision, and the central figure of all, the old dame herself! One windy morning, however, when creeping slowly to school, we were told that our old mentor was dead, which sad tidings—in the prospect, probably, of escaping from the thraldom of the school room—set us all rejoicing. Such is childhood!

For generations our family had been of the same trade—that is, boot and shoe makers—as I learned from an elder cousin. It originated, as he stated, in a family of five brothers and two sisters, some two centuries before. Thomas, who was a shoemaker, built the house in which I was born. Of the four other brothers, one was a cooper, another a woolstapler, another a farmer, and the fourth a banker, having been manager for many years of the old or Cobbe's bank at Banbury. Thus from this simple ancestry, it will be seen that for two centuries my father's forelders had lived entirely by trade.

I was about seven years old when "granny" died; and I well recollect the funeral, at which we all followed in village fashion. We had an undertaker, who brought us lutestring and crape paste board bonnets, and we had new black merino dresses. A fussy nurse, who dressed us all upstairs for the funeral procession, told us what we had to do, and how to behave ourselves. When we had got our gloves on and were nearly ready, she brought us white pocket handkerchiefs, which we, as children, had not been used to have. When she came to me, I asked her what it was for. "Oh, to cry with, to be sure," she said. "They'll all have them, and you must do as the others do."

"But I shall not cry," I said, "and so I shall not want it." But she persisted that I must have it, if only for a make belief to hold up to my eyes. This was enough. Realistic child as I was (she most likely called me an obstinate one), I positively refused to take it. But I was often called "queer and like nobody else," by women we had about the house, who were not used to my wanting to know the reason why of everything.

That funeral left us a troubled family. We had now to leave the old ancestral home, which had become endeared to us by long years of joys and sorrows. To it my father had brought home two happy brides, with whom he had spent years of peace; and there children had been born to him, that had endeared their union, and brought joy and gladness to their hearth. There also in the early days of his married life had he, under the blessed influence of that religion—which created all things new, which makes crooked things straight and rough places even—bowed his knee in prayer as a regenerate man, in the presence of that holy Being on whose side he had solemnly decided to stand and serve for the rest of his life. There also he had great sorrows, which had had their sanctifying uses in keeping him true to God and heaven. From this house his first wife had been borne to the silent grave, and a little boy of some four years old (drowned in the canal) had soon been laid beside her.

Now the dear old memories were to be broken, the dear old associations scattered as by a sudden stroke. Some of my father's relatives were very different people to himself, vindictive and covetous, who thought nothing of annoying him and putting him to all sorts of inconvenience. For long months we were a troubled household; they wanting to get possession of the house, and we having none to go to. At length, however, a comfortable family residence, with large garden and orchard, and two or three cottages attached, was to be sold in the upper part of the village. This my father bought; and with many alterations, and some necessary additions, it became our final family home.

At this new house we were pleasantly accommodated, not, it is true, with any pretentions to gentility, as it was only a thatched one; but my father after awhile, as he was able to afford it, had the roof taken off, and the house raised and slated. The roses and honeysuckle clustering in fragrance and homely beauty over its walls, consecrating long years of dear peaceful happy life, we as children once spent within it. The Puritans, indeed, were not, so far as I ever knew them, either a gloomy or morose kind of people.

For the first time in my life I became acquainted with song singing, from a washerwoman, who came once a month to do the "big" wash. She was a merry sort of a woman, with twinkling eyes; and was always ready to be coaxed to do anything for my gratification, though she knew it was not allowed. She would put on a grave face in a moment, if my father happened to open the back kitchen door, and enquire who she had there, which he often did, knowing my liking for Bet's songs, I suppose. Indeed, I have known her try to hide me behind the big tubs, saying, "No, master," in answer to his enquiries, pretending after, when I rose up from my little stool, that she did not know I was there

All this I knew to be wrong, but still found my way to the kitchen when she was there, as she had a great store of songs popular at that time, but quite

new to me, which I delighted to hear. She sang
them with a clear lilting voice, without much tune,
for which I did not care. I could hear every word,
and soon got them all by heart. Thus "The Lass
of Richmond Hill," "The Gallant Hussar," "Rory
O' More," "Sweet Jenny Jones," Bailey's charming
"Isle of Beauty" and "I'd be a Butterfly," and
others came to be known to me, and dearly loved.
Often when the washerwoman was working late I
would sit in the kitchen, on winter nights, on a low
stool, pretending to be watching potatoes roasting
under the copper; but in reality to get Bet to sing
me all the old songs over again, entreating her
often to sing very low, lest my father, who was in
the shop, might hear. This she did to please me,
satisfied most likely at my childish liking for her
songs, which none of the other children seemed to
care much about.

Poor woman! many years after, when I was at
my father's house on a visit, she came to see me
"once more," as she said, but time had indeed
wrought changes in her. The once merry twinkling
eyes had both been taken out, leaving hollow empty
eyeless sockets, over which lay her folded locks of

mournful grey hair. The subdued expression of the features seeming to express submission to God's will, all so changed and altered from what she was when she lilted merrily over her washing-tub. Such is our life! But I owe it to her to say, that for good or ill, she was one of my early teachers in the matter of verse, which, whether in hymn or song, from childhood always fascinated me.

But during this troubled period, when I was about seven years old, I had been sent for a few months to another dame school, where I learned to knit and sew, the sole object for which I attended. It was a parish school, and was visited by ladies from the vicarage. It was kept, as most village schools were kept then, by a woman, who, by some disease or other was unable to move from her chair or lift her hand to her mouth. Yet she had a robust look as she sat from morning till night in the large chair, her great white stick, which reached to any part of the cottage floor in which the school was held, standing constantly beside her.

Her knowledge was very small. The girls had a lesson once a day in the New Testament, and the little ones read out of the "Reading Made Easy."

But knitting and sewing occupied nearly the whole time of the girls, who perhaps might average from nine to ten. I was a diviner of spirits even then, and did not admire the mistress. I saw she was passionate and partial and very pharisaical. I do not remember to have had any lessons there. I could read well enough any book at that time, thanks to my inordinate appetite for knowledge.

One day the ladies came, and called up all the readers in the Testament, and I had to stand up with the others. After reading two or three chapters, the ladies proposed to ask us some questions, which they did, of a very easy kind. I stood and returned answers to everything they asked, no one else, easy as they were, even trying to do so.

When all was over, as was natural, the ladies asked who this little girl was who had answered so well. The mistress told them my father's name, and the significant exclamation was, "But he does not attend church!" Hence it followed that I had no commendation. I was, however, promised a reward, which I afterwards received in the shape of a New Testament. But for all that, it was evident I was looked upon as an alien. They never condescended to speak to me whenever they came; and I on my part was, I fear, too reserved in the matter of behaviour, taking a delight in omitting the profound curtsies which the village children never dared to miss giving, when any of the vicar's family came into the school, or appeared anywhere in the street. I did not learn this from my father, who ever spoke in the most respectful and conciliating manner to any of them.

Settled in our new home, I was at once taken from this school, having acquired the useful arts of knitting and sewing there, for which I had been sent. I was now a girl of eight years of age, with a great love of books and a very good capacity for reading. My poor mother looked upon reading, even when I was a little child, as a species of idleness; very well for Sundays or evenings, when baby was asleep and I was not wanted for anything else. As a last resource mother would tell my father. But dear, good, loving father, as he was, always took my part on this point, saying, "If the child does nothing worse than that, it is not very bad." Then addressing me, he would say, "My little wench, you must mind and hear when your mother calls, and do what she bids you. There will be time enough for reading afterwards."

In my earliest years, I used to spend my half-pence at the small lollipop shop in the village, in buying "Cinderella," always a delight to me, "The Babes in the Wood," "Jack the Giant Killer," etc. These I read clandestinely. I early acquired a sense of what was considered wrong in this direction at home. I was always a solitary child; could play alone dressing dolls, or at ball, or hop-scotch, in which I delighted. I often stayed playing by myself on some paving stones in the churchyard, through which I went to school, making myself much later in getting home than I ought to have done.

But whatever I did, I always felt that my father was right, and what he did not allow or approve was wrong. His rule was my law of right, and my conscience was established on that practical law of Right, which I saw every day enforced with fewest words into his life. In regarding his word, I regarded an absolute and unimpeachable authority, which I never doubted; and perhaps the real worth of religion to nations as well as to individuals, might be found in the true rule of the family. In fact, true religion constrains loving allegiance, as it did in our home; all of us being united in common love toward our father.

It was about this time that I was sent to a higher grade school, kept by two ladies, at the wharf. Cropredy wharf was on the Oxford canal, which flows through there; the wharfinger at that time being a Mr. H., who with his two daughters, Miss H. and Mrs. B., and her young son, occupied a large square brick built house at the wharf. The two ladies kept a school of some pretensions, having a few boarders, and at which all the farmer's and tradesmen's daughters in the villages around, were educated. This family at the wharf were Methodists of the truest type. The father, a true christian gentleman; and his eldest daughter, Miss H., forever remaining in my memory as the highest example of an intelligent christian lady it has been my lot to know personally. She was, perhaps, indescribable —not at all beautiful, but slender, stately, self-possessed, and lady-like, with a sweet, generous, condescending smile.

Even now, when more than half a century has

passed away, how vividly I can see that sweetly natural, yet saintly face, worn with pain and suffering, over which she seemed ever to triumph; as also that of the father, whose snowy white head and calm, dignified, yet patient face, always impressed me as something of the divine. His words were few and very quiet, but always kind. There was no pomp nor pride. He never thought of what his dues were from others; could not, as his kindness was the same alike to all, both rich and poor. His placid smile fell on all alike. He was everywhere and always the same, as when on Sundays he reverently stood up to worship with his face to the wall in the small Methodist chapel in the village.

So I was sent to this school at the wharf, very much to my heart's delight. Correct and lady-like manners were considered to be almost the be all and end all of a girl's education. This great and absorbing attention to manners, new as it was to me then, attracted my attention, and commanded my respect. At our home, gravity, order, submission to elders, and respect to superiors, were enforced; but we were taught to obey and do what was right because it was so.

But though I continually made mistakes and often forgot myself, I had always a great admiration for persons possessing and practising excellent manners, and rarely formed a friendship with any one in my after life who was not blest with this accomplishment. Human nature pays for cultivation, and good behaviour beautifies childhood and youth, as well as dignifies age. I seemed in a new world with companions reduced to such fine orderliness, such prompt attention, such willing obedience. But rigid rule was enforced upon all, notwithstanding appearances.

It was indeed a very good school; thoroughness being the aim in the few things that were professed to be taught, as well as almost faultless discipline and good manners. A girl's education at that time consisted principally of needlework of various descriptions, from plain sewing to all manner of fancy work and embroidery, including muslin and net, on which we worked or flowered squares for the shoulders, veils, caps, collars, and borders; likewise a multitude of things not in wear now, but then considered very necessary. Parents were prouder then of their daughters' pieces of nedlework than of their scholarship.

I believe my father would have wished it different, but it was usual to consign a pupil to the sole care of the governess, to direct and guide as she might deem fit and proper. So I was educated according to her idea, not his; the only exception made being that I might be specially put forward in arithmetic, which was done accordingly. Every afternoon, therefore, Miss H., my favourite teacher, came to the school room door and called me to her in the sitting room, where she sat with her father, and there in that blessed quietude, with my kind teacher's help, I unravelled the mysteries of long division and compound addition, quite as much as it was thought necessary then for girls to know. Arithmetic was much more thoroughly taught to girls in Scotland and the North of England, and in most other branches of learning, as I found some years after. A blessing it was, that at this school we got no frivolous notions of life and its great duties, and that we had before us living examples of the sweet influences of religion and morality.

My special delight was in the learning, small as it was, that was then taught. I took much interest in flowering net and embroidering muslin, but less

in canvas work, at which I was always slow. But
we all travelled through one groove, however diverse
our tastes might be.   Thus I did an endless quantity
of embroidery and flowering, children's caps, muslin
aprons, and many other things ; as well as a teapot
stand, with a tiger in the middle !   The canvas of
the last article being very fine, I drew it up and
spoilt it, and had to begin afresh, which cost me
many tears.

What long months I worked at it—and how I
hated it—but it was all in vain ! For long years
Englishwomen's souls were almost as sorely crippled
and cramped by the devices of the school room, as
the Chinese women's feet by their shoes.   I had to
go on with this hateful employment.   "It must be
done, and done well," I was told, which I fully
realized.   I never remember to have been praised
for any work I did, though I did a great deal.

But I had my delight in going early into the
school room, while the rest were at play, sitting in
its grateful quietude, reading over and over again
such class books as the "Pleasing Instructor,"
Magnall's "Questions," Goldsmith's "History of
England," etc., all new to me.   The "Pleasing

Instructor" I liked very much. It contained a selection of articles from the best English authors— Addison, Steele, Dryden, Young, Pope, the Taylors, etc. Hitherto I had had no opportunity of reading such books. Any I could get hold of being for the most part children's books, with the exception of religious ones, such as Boston's "Crook in the Lot," Doddridge's "Rise and Progress," and others, which I had duly pondered to try to make them out, not always with success.

But here was a book I had a faculty for. These authors wrote from their hearts for humanity, and I could follow them fully and with delight, though but a child. They awakened my young nature, and I found for the first time that my pondering heart was akin to that of the whole human race. And when I read the famous essays of Steele and Addison, I could realize much of their truth and beauty of expression. Poetry in the form of songs and hymns had, almost as an infant, attracted me. Pope's stanzas, which I read at school as an eight year old child, showed me how far I felt and shared the sentiment that he wrote, when he says,

Thus let me live unseen, unknown,
　　Thus unlamented let me die ;
Steal from the world, and not a stone
　　Tell where I lie.

I had no companions, or at that time very few.
I never talked of reading, though when I went into
the cottages I hung over their quaint old pictures,
and their few tattered books, such as the "Seven
Champions of Christendom," "The Good and Bad
Angel," and old Catholic legends, about which I
had a world of questions to ask. One intelligent
woman I specially remember, who had seen better
days, and whose parents had been Roman Catholics.
From her I got many an old legend and story, and
she it was who first told me of monks and nuns and
abbots.

I used to like to sit by her table, and, while she
was busy doing up pasteboard bonnets, ask her
questions about the old Catholics and their times,
of whom, before, I had known nothing. I liked to
hear her stories, which interested me deeply, for
"Mary Gardner" was no common woman. Not
that she herself was a Catholic. At that time she
attended the same chapel as my father did, and was
a woman who had passed through many afflictions.

Many of her old adages I well remember, especially one in reference to our impatience about the rain, which kept us indoors. At such times she would say, "Hold your tongues, children! It's raining victuals to-day!" I put this phrase into verse many years after, and published it in the papers.

CHAPTER III.

ONE of my Sunday-school teachers at this time won my admiration. Though only a young man, he was so sincere and devout a Methodist, that he was universally respected, and acknowledged even by the wickedest, to be what he professed to be. I went to the Methodist Sunday-school in the village, near my own home. One Sunday morning, I do not know how it occurred, another girl and myself transgressed in something, probably in laughter. I never could resist the infection of that sort of thing; and as the teacher was a strict disciplinarian, we were ordered to remain when the others were dismissed.

All having gone, he called us before him, and in the tenderest tones asked if we would remember for the future, that the all-seeing eye of God beheld us. With tears of deep contrition, I took his proffered hand, and determinedly answered "Yes."

Then he knelt down with us, and in deep and fervid utterances, in which tears choked his voice at times, he prayed that we might be kept true to God and our promise, and from ever falling into sin again. I left him, a sadder but a wiser child, always regarding his deep prayer as one of my first religious experiences, and ever after regarding him with affectionate reverence as one wholly good.

I have recorded this simple incident as having, in after life, very much influenced my own mind in punishing any of my pupils. I saw that the good effects of punishment result entirely from the calm, pure, loving spirit in which it is administered. My teacher's punishment made me a better girl; roused my thoughts to the evil of doing as others do, and made me feel sorry that I had given others pain. So when it came to be my own turn, many years after, to stand at the head of a school, I invariably adhered to the practice of keeping delinquents in school for a short time after the rest had gone, to any other mode of punishment, finding by this method I could better effect a kindly alliance with the offender.

In proof of this, I once remember telling a girl

of ten or eleven to write a verse after all were gone,
for some fault committed, and having spoken a few
earnest words to her, I left the room.   On coming
back, I took her slate expecting to find the verse—
but it was not so.   She had written, in the form of
a child's letter, her deep sorrow at having grieved
me, and promised to do so no more.   On seeing
me reading it, she threw her arms around my neck,
and shed a flood of tears.   I kissed her and wept
also.

This shows that the events of my childhood
made a deep impression on me; that I was a keen
observer, in after years adopting what I thought
was good; and, above all, that a deeply religious
character always attracted my veneration.   Punish-
ments were then different in ladies' schools, as in
the one I attended for example.   To stand erect in
a corner for an hour; to wear a frightfully ugly
dunce's cap, standing on a stool; and similar chas-
tisements were constantly occurring.   Once only I
occupied the stool.

Some ill-natured school girl fixed upon me the
making of a great noise, while the governess was
out.   As a punishment I was set on the stool, with

this horrible cap on my head, opposite the window. A sensitive child, I was overwhelmed with grief, especially as I was quite innocent; but in vain I protested. I was not even noticed, which injustice —child as I was—I thought the worst part of all. At last, seeing how dreadfully I cried, a little girl stepped up to the governess, and with a deep curtsy, said that I did not make any noise, but was sitting reading on the form (my usual custom).

I was then taken down; but I never forgot it. It was a hateful ordeal, robbing a child of its self-respect, which should always be kept inviolate, if at all possible. I remained at this school for several years. I liked it well; revolting against nothing but the endless fancy work that I was made to do.

However, to my great delight, one day my father came home, saying he had been at a sale, and had bought a lot of old books. They were duly brought, and laid down on the floor; a lot of tattered books of all descriptions; novels, histories, poems, plays (including some of Shakespeare's). He had surely thought of his little girl, who was so fond of books, for he was too busy to look them over. He ordered them to be taken up into the attic. But as soon as unnoticed, I began to examine and purloin some of them, hiding them away for future use. I read the batch I retained with great delight, finding books or parts of books of a description quite new to any I had read before.

Especially I remember an old copy of Kirke White's "Remains," which I read over and over with great delight; and, perhaps, from him and Shakespeare, I learned to love classical poetry. My delight, which I kept to myself, was inexpressible. I never said anything to anybody about my love of books, always feeling rather condemned than otherwise about it. Whenever I had done what work I was set to do, my chief pleasure was to slip away unobserved into some quiet spot, where all unseen I could read till the last glimmer of day was lost in the lonely night. Often and often on wet evenings, or on Saturday afternoons, when released from household work, I would creep quietly up to the attic where the books were kept, which was entered by a trap door.

So time ran on, and though I was taunted by

nearly all the family, except my father, as being "always reading," I did, in reality, a great deal beside, for ours was a busy house, and idleness was a thing not to be tolerated in any one of us. In books, or work, or healthful play, our first years were certainly passed, and perhaps this was the reason why in after years, I could always lay the most fascinating book down at any moment.

In the winter evenings, we had all something to do; and my lot was mostly to go with my father to the leather room, and hold the candle for light while he cut the thick cow-hides into soles for boots and shoes. Many a kind word did he give me on these occasions, asking after my school work, and guiding and encouraging me as to what I should do. Blessed times they always were, and full of instruction! I ran willingly with him, knowing he would tell me all manner of pleasant things; what I should try to do, and what avoid; speaking to me rather as a woman than as a girl; quite aware of all my odd ways.

Early I became the companion of my father, still hanging on his hand, and walking with him to his chapel at Great Bourton on fine Sundays, which was a mile off; and as I grew older, to the other places around, to hear special sermons, to missionary meetings, public breakfasts, soirees, etc.

So when yet a girl, I heard the great missionary, William Knibb, describe the freeing of the slaves in the isle of Jamaica, on the memorable first of August, which I shall never forget. I still remember well how intensely I listened, though my feet would not yet reach the floor from the high pewed seat. I can see that brown emotional face yet, as he told the pathetic story of the liberation, and how they watched the hours together till midnight; how he and the other missionaries marched in procession at the head of the liberated slaves, to a grave which had been dug, and into which grave each one cast his chains and fetters, with shouts of joy and triumph. He told also, with glowing features, of numerous processions, on the first free day, through the towns, in which the women tossed their babes in their arms as they danced and shouted—and the great missionary concluded by saying, "And I should have danced too, if I had only known how!" This address was delivered at Banbury, about four miles from our home.

The nonconformists of these times had a passion for hearing noted preachers; and my father knowing my delight in this special class of oratory, often took me with him to hear some celebrity of this kind, the distance sometimes being so great that even by hanging on his arm, I could hardly get along, I was so tired. So I heard Eustace Carey, Howard Hinton, Dr. Franklin of Coventry, and others; also a remarkable sermon preached by a Welsh nonconformist, named Jenkin Thomas. In those quiet days we talked of such things in the country for weeks together.

Soon after this time, a cousin of ours died, and my father bought an old four-wheel pony trap. In this conveyance a party of us often went together to meetings. Occasionally, too, we visited my own mother's family in Gloucestershire, with whom, as they were nearly all Baptists, we had a close and constant intercourse. My uncle Newth, a small farmer, corresponded with my father, mostly in rhyme. His rhyming letters, as I always remember, were hailed with great delight by us all. They were read aloud by my father, to our great delight, till

we became quite intimate with them, and were able
to repeat certain parts.

My mother's sisters and their families, all farmers
—Charles Newth and Cornelius Farmiloe—attended
Shortwood chapel, Nailsworth, a very large Baptist
chapel, with stabling and out-houses for horses and
conveyances. Connected with it was a fine burying
ground, where my uncle Farmiloe had a vault, in
which his family were buried. They often had
eminent Baptist ministers and missionaries at Shortwood. My uncle Newth wrote to my father on one
occasion:

> I wish you'd been here the first Sabbath in June,
> We had Pearce from Calcutta, both morning and noon,
> And likewise a Burchell to swell out the tune
> Of worthy the Lamb that was slain.

By these rhyming letters we were all set rhyming.
My father often essaying to write back in rhyme.
An old and dear nonconformist friend of my father's,
an educated and intelligent man, a Mr. George
Atkins, who attended at Bourton chapel, sometimes wrote rhyming letters to my father and
Uncle Newth. I still remember a bit of his rhyme,
in the form of a note to my father who had asked
him to dinner.

With your kind invitation, I could not comply,
If you read these lines, they'll tell you for why;
The loss of my pocket book filled me with care,
The rascals bereaved me at Banbury fair.

Hearing these letters and notes read, I got to write bits and scraps of rhymes, while yet a girl. I remember writing valentines for my sister and one of her companions. A gay young fellow persisted in paying his addresses, which they wished to cease; and to try to effect their purpose I wrote some repellant rigmarole ending thus—

With your dandy hat and boots so fine,
You shall never be my valentine.

This was my first essay in rhyming for a purpose, and was kept strictly secret from all but those interested. My uncle's rhyming letters gave me the first impulse. We all admired him, not only for his rhyming abilities, but for his stern nonconformist principles, in the defence of which he never wanted either a rhyme or a reason.

Happy times we all had at our house, when my uncle and one or two of my cousins came to see us, travelling out of Gloucestershire in some big lumbering old conveyance, over cross country roads, and in some places where there were no roads at all. It was always late in the day when they came, but we had good fires and pleasant welcomes for them. As for conversation, these religious folks reaped harvests that supplied talk everywhere, both profitable and pleasing ; and their anecdotes and stories were endless, often, I fear, told at the expense of some luckless clergyman or his more luckless clerk. Our relatives stayed with us, on these occasions, for a few days or a week. Then our house put on its best garniture, everything, though plain and humble, being very clean ; and all was good humour and good behaviour.

In a country home like ours, we had a great delight in seeing fresh places. I early got a love of fine scenery, from my father pointing out the hills and Druidical stones of Rollright, the hamlet of Burdrop, and other places, as we travelled into Gloucestershire, etc. But through all these years I was still, as ever, a book worm, rummaging for books wherever I went. So whatever book I found I read, good or bad, keeping hid the doubtful ones from every one's sight. In this way I remember reading the life of Doctor Faustus, which I dared not let anyone see, with the story of his traffic with the Evil one, and how he helped him to the invention of printing, especially of the Bible !

I also got acquainted—how I can hardly tell—with a broken down family who had kept the "Brazen Nose" inn, in the village. They were not exactly such people as were approved of at our house ; but in looking over their house I found they had a great many old books, which they said had been left by travellers staying at the inn. Any of these they kindly lent me, and among them were a great many I had never seen, mostly novels, but some of them very good ones. There I found the "Vicar of Wakefield," the "Exiles of Siberia," the "Castle of Otranto," and many others, including, as I remember, some Methodist biographies, all of which I devoured voraciously.

The vicar was a haughty man, and fully believed in his right to rule the consciences of the parishioners, but he rarely interfered with us. Nevertheless, there were exceptional times, and I remember one day, just after an early dinner, the vicar opening our street door—the rule then—standing with it in his hand, and asking if we had not one or two children old enough to be confirmed, as the bishop was coming for that purpose. My father, who was sitting in his arm-chair by the fire, rose to receive him, saying, "I have learned from the New Testament that the apostles confirmed 'the christians,' and must just say, when my children are old enough to understand such things, they must judge for themselves."

At this the vicar flew into a great passion, and stamped on the floor, saying, "You will never do as other people do." To this my father replied, "In anything else, sir, in which I can oblige you, I shall be glad to do so; but my children must decide for themselves." With this his reverence slammed the door, and went away without any word of courtesy. My poor father looked tried and put about on these occasions; but I as a child witnessing such haughtiness and passion on the part of a minister of religion, felt all my young spirit in revolt against a church, whose minister came to the people in the name of pride and passion and custom, rather than in the spirit of Christ; striving as a pope to overbear and overawe, rather than as a christian minister to instruct and enlighten.

Once when a child, on my governess setting me to learn the church catechism, my father had written all round the margin of the book, "Popery! Popery! please don't let the child learn this." This I saw to my consternation, when I went up to her the next morning, and at which she smiled as she closed the book. Things of this kind, in due time, became clearer to my apprehension, and helped to make me a sturdy nonconformist to the end of my days, as my father had been before me.

CHAPTER IV.

BUT many things in our old way of life now came to an end. My father, in consequence of business losses, had twice canvassed for the office of relieving officer and registrar of the district; the second time with success, notwithstanding his dissent. This had led to his giving up all his ordinary business. My eldest brother and I were consequently placed in a shop which had been previously taken on the Oxford canal in the village, to which the shoemaking business was likewise to be joined. We were both young for such an important undertaking. The serious ways of our home life, somewhat intensified by family trouble, probably added more than a share of deep thoughtfulness to my youthful appearance, which led strangers to suppose me older than I really was. My woman's life in reality commenced from then, and I might even say before then, for I divined, if I did not tell all the family secrets, and shared all its sad troubles.

How deeply thankful we all felt for my father's election to the ill-paid post of relieving officer. I well remember our regarding it as a special providence, as an intervention of the Highest on our behalf, the sudden turning of the clergy, his sworn foes, to vote for him. There was no loud singing of Te Deums at our house, but much quiet and devout thanksgiving, unheard by any human ears. It was early spring. Ash Wednesday followed the week after, and we were all surprised to hear my father say he was going to church. I always shall see the reverent devout form standing erect there, giving all the responses, without book. At last coming to the Magnificat, then, with the full emphasis of a truly thankful heart, he lifted up his voice, and said, "My soul doth magnify the Lord, and my spirit hath rejoiced in God my Saviour, for he that is mighty hath magnified me, and holy is His name."

It seemed as if he had come there to show his gratitude before the congregation, and to testify with devout heart what great things God had done for him. This may seem a small matter, but it has always seemed to me an honourable struggle with poverty. Unpaid bills were an intolerable burden at our house, to be ended the soonest possible way, not by modern bankruptcy, but by honestly paying them. In this way, in a few years, every bill was met, and though we were never rich, the family honour was never soiled by unpaid bills. In his new office, which he held for twenty-one years, by persistent thrift and diligence, he cleared everything, and had a trifle to leave us all at his death. Long and reverently I could linger over the memory of my dear father, the best man whom I have ever known, the one still the best loved of my life.

> My boast is not that I deduce my birth
> From loins enthroned, or rulers of the earth ;
> But higher far my proud pretensions rise—
> The heir of parents passed into the skies.

My life had now become a very busy and responsible one, for one so young ; but I had profited by our family troubles, and my brother agreed with me that we must refuse credit to all doubtful customers. So our shop soon righted itself. My brother led the men in his own department, and with little guidance I managed the grocery and provision shop. In the intervals of custom I did much, if not all, in the house, as well as keeping the books.   Finally, I got handy and expert in making articles of wearing apparel, dresses for myself and younger sisters ; indeed, anything to save expense.   My brother and I did all manner of things to advance our tardy fortunes.   He kept bees and pigs; and I kept poultry, which latter brought me in a certain amount of pocket money. Work was indeed our life, and so anxious and conscientious was I, that I soon got to make children's frocks, both for our own family and others, by sitting up late in the evenings.

Once I remember—on one of these nights— to have seen a poor young fellow buried, at twelve o'clock at night, in the outskirts of the churchyard, in front of our shop.   There was then no christian burial for the poor suicide; no bell was rung nor service said, nor any of the beautiful formulas of the Church of England burial service used.   A few poor men (perhaps his brothers), with horn lanterns let him down into his silent grave, as I saw standing at our door; while afterwards the heavy clods of earth which rolled rapidly down over the coffin, in the silent night, seemed awfully weird and melancholy. Thank God there have been and still are human hearts in this great world, who have changed all this; and the poor suicide is now reverently pitied, and has sweet words of holy hope said over his forlorn grave.

This hard work was good for me. I felt that I was useful and helpful; too much engaged for harbouring idle thoughts or vain dreams, yet still cherishing aspirations after something beyond the limits of my power of definition, or the depth of my dreams. But this did not make me unhappy. It kept me silent, reserved, shy, and without any desire for intimacies with thoughtless, gay girls. My friends at this time were a few of my old schoolfellows, in better circumstances than myself, who persisted in their attachments to me. I was still the managing spirit in all our childish schemes of amusement at their big farm houses, or excursions on long summer evenings, or on holiday afternoons over the farm, or up the sweet bowery rural roads in quest of violets or primroses, or the more delicate cowslip, which, (obeying the mandates of the mothers,) we gathered in large handfuls for making cowslip wine of.

Very delightful to me were these rambles through the sweetly scented lanes in spring, when fields were rich with gay flowers, the beauty of the year. Pleasant undying memories have ever hung around them. They attracted us together then : and now all my old school companions are dead but one, who is in South America. Fifty years ago she became the wife of a young man, whose father left him a plantation on condition that he would go there and live on it. I feel that that was the only pleasurable period of my whole life, having nothing in it vile or selfish; the sole object in all our schemes being to carry out some idea of childish fun.

O happy time of childhood ! when small troubles enhance future pleasures—pleasures which are the one abiding joy of a long life ! Before the jealousies and envies of life begin, all is new and untried, and neither they nor I saw far into the great life of the world, or thought for one moment that the things we had read thereof in books were not true. One girl, whom I loved very much, and who had the rarest roses on her cheeks, was the first to fall. She became a faded memory, with a name written merely on a grand stone in a village churchyard. Another and yet another of these bright young girls, did I, with six others, all dressed in pure white, according to the custom of the time and place, help to carry to their graves. The old churchyard has many mementoes of bright school friends who have perished in the march of life.

All my old friends, who came to see me in the first years at the shop, marvelled at my busy life. Still as time flew by, and I became seventeen, bits of romance crept into my life, as is common to all of human kind. Yet even here I was hardly like the rest. I objected then, as all my life long, to women lowering themselves to coarse jesting, loud laughing, and especially to the objectionable rudeness of village youths and maidens. Shy and silent and reserved in my manners, I was much offended at all looseness of behaviour in others. I thought then, as I have taught ever since, that a woman can be a lady without money, and that parents and teachers should prompt her to be this truly in the interest of morality and virtue.

The washerwoman and other women we had about our house, when I was a girl, used to say,

"Mary must have a minister. She reads so much, and is so grave, and can tell you all about things." And I think I liked the idea, though I said nothing. But I had neither time nor inclination to think of these things at the shop. My one ambition was to get our family free from debt. So while other girls at my age were an expense to their parents, I am free to say that I rendered mine all the assistance in my power. I was not without selfishness either, and liked to exact whatever respect I could from the rude element which surrounded me.

My brother had a friend who oftener came home with him than I liked, and who brought things as presents which I was too shy to reject, though I showed they gave me no pleasure. As he was a lad of good prospects, my father spoke to me about him one day. He said I surely could find something to say to him, adding, he would like to see me with someone who really cared for me. To this I replied, I did not want him, and could work for myself. Quite true, but not quite easy, as I afterwards found out. Yet I never regretted my action.

My father had always been fond of having minis-ters about us. We had them often calling and stopping to tea or dinner. One Baptist minister from Gloucestershire sometimes stayed for weeks together, going away on Sundays to preach at various chapels, while waiting a "call." He was a clever man, from Shortwood, who finally settled at Northampton. I once went with my father, in our old trap, to spend a Sabbath with him and his family at that place. The first railway in those parts was then in course of formation; and I remember we called to see it on our way home.

This Mr. Ashmead, the minister, had anecdotes for evermore of his student life at Bristol, under Isaiah Birt and others, familiar to Baptist ears. One I recollect of a certain youth, named Caleb, who was a great talker, and very fond of spending his evenings in some pleasant friend's house, and getting let in by some friendly student after hours. One dark night after the usual signal, the door opened, and Caleb skipped in as usual, turning a pirouette as he snapped his fingers with the words, "Nick'd it again, Caleb!" when the voice beside him said quietly, "Not so fast, young man. Isaiah has nick'd Caleb this time!" It was the principal himself, who having got wind of the thing, had sat up on purpose to give the student a surprise.

One fine summer afternoon, not long after we had been at the shop, as I sat by the window, the Hon. W. Parker—who was canvassing the county of Oxfordshire for Parliamentary votes—suddenly sprang into the house, by the open door, and stood before me with a train of gentlemen (the village freeholders) behind him. A tall, handsome young man, wearing a white hat, which he did not take off—he enquired for my father, who had a vote for the county. I stood up in my schoolgirl way, with gravity and respect, and replied my father was not at home. He said he wanted my father to vote for him, and as he was out, he urged me to speak for him. I stood silent. He then began to coax me; and in a moment, before I knew what was going to happen, he kissed me, and fled! Bewildered and indignant, I resumed my seat; but, young as I was, all my nature rose in revolt against him. His presumption offended me most acutely. I felt I was not an ignorant nor a giddy girl, to be pleased with any such undue liberties.

Possibly this little incident helped in after years, to make me more energetic in my speech and writings against the insidious treachery of the

Tories. Many a strong letter did I pen in Carlisle, against Tory tactics and disestablishment, which I hope helped to show those who read them, something of their fallacious and misleading pretensions.

There was a great need of an earnest minister in our village ; but sad to say, as is often the case in factory towns, the rude element of drunkenness and riot, oftener becomes one of scorn and opposition than of penitence and religious conviction. So it was in our village. A son of one of the old dissenting families, who regularly attended the chapel, had become awfully dissipated ; had left his father's comfortable home, and become a sad drunken sot, unfit for any decent society. Every effort made to reclaim him had failed. Well do I remember, one Sunday morning, the quiet chapel being fluttered in the midst of the service by the once bright, well dressed youth coming in, and making his way to the top of the gallery—a fearful prodigal—without hat, or coat, or waistcoat, or shoes, or stockings !

I had for two or three years been deeply impressed that my life of indecision was wrong. I felt that my apathy to religion was not right. At times, I very much condemned myself for my novel reading, which I knew my father would utterly condemn. I more than once vowed to give it up, but never did. Indeed, one evening I went to the extent of shutting myself in my bedroom, and there writing down a number of resolutions as to my future conduct, which, alas! I never kept.

Our chapel at Great Bourton was up a lonely road, between two villages, yet whatever the weather might be, or whenever the chapel doors might be open in the dark wet nights of winter, I was sure to be there, often with a sad desponding heart. I hoped some good word spoken there might bring me light and peace from on High, For this end I continually prayed, though I said nothing to any one, nor did any intrusive religious friend, as they do among the Methodists, try to probe my wounds, and tempt my utterances on the subject. My father's religion was pre-eminently a silent one, and the people at this little chapel were all of them very much so, though still of the kindest. Pleasant quiet smiles, and kind "How do you do's," they all had, as in country fashion they swayed your hand affectionately horizontally backward and forward, enquiring for friends at home, or making apt remarks about the weather.

Then, as in Cromwell's time, the big clouds of despondency and contrition darkened the spirit for months, often till the still small voice of mercy and forgiveness, like a ray of sunshine out of a heavy sky, cleared the vision, and made every sound become one of glad hope and blessing. So I kept on my way through this dark time, saying no word to any one, not even to my brother, who, like me, was on his way to the wicket gate. We had both been very much impressed with those Sinai thunders, those terrors of the law, which we had heard in the sermons of our young preacher. I remember my brother rising from his chair one Sunday night, and saying seriously, "Shall we have a few words of prayer, before we go to bed?" I had been longing to say the same thing, but was deterred by my old shyness, and therefore acquiesced with silent gladness.

A decided mystic as I have been all my life, I at this time doubtless was passing through some of its inexpressible phases, and found deeps within deeps of what seemed to me inextinguishable sorrow, for as Goethe sings :

Who ne'er his bread in sorrow ate,
Who never spent the midnight hours
Weeping and wishing for the morrow,
He knows you not, ye heavenly powers.

In the winter, when the snow lay thick on the ground, I have known my father send me word from his room by mother, not to think of setting out till he was up, and able to go with me. Otherwise, in a usual way, I rose early on Sunday mornings, and went with my brother to the early prayer meetings, held at eight o'clock. These walks were very pleasant through the spring and summer, when all around was fair and beautiful, but in the winter when no foot had invaded the lonely roads after a deep snow, or in the cruel winds or pouring rains of late autumn—through which we went nothing daunted—they were different. So much so, that an atheistic farmer, whose gate we passed, used to say we were "mad." Be that as it may, it was the most divine infatuation I ever felt, and of which I never once relented or grew weary. I gave up all. The earrings were taken out of my ears, the coral necklace laid aside, and the flowers and bows from my bonnet. It was a joy to me to give them up. Saint Theresa could not have delighted more in the cross than I did.   I had, in fact, learnt that grandest of all lessons, to low lie in the Lord's hands, and to feel that every step downward is a step upward.   Till then I had never known how sweet life was, bereft of all its ambitions and earthly strivings.

CHAPTER V.

A GREATER sorrow than I had ever before known now befel me. I was cut off from my old busy life of the shop. Things had improved, and my brother had married. After staying a few weeks to put everything in order, and initiate his wife into the mysteries of shopkeeping, I went home again to my father's house, as he desired. I had worked hard, but had had no wages. Few girls in their teens worked so self-denyingly and resolutely as I did then. I knew, indeed, the worst was past; and in a few years the family ship righted itself, every bill being eventually paid, and every account settled But for myself, as is often the case with women, even the most capable and energetic, the one small event of my brother's marrying had stranded me without occupation.

The September following, I was publicly baptised by immersion, with ten others, my brother and the minister being among the number. Like the minister, we were under conviction of the scriptural obligation of this rite and mode of its administration; and resolute to fulfil all righteousness, I had become enamoured of the idea that I should thus publicly witness my attachment to my dear Lord and Saviour. We were baptised by the minister of the chapel, before all the congregation, in the morning of the first Sabbath in the month. In the afternoon, I sat down for the first time with the members of the church, to the ordinance of the Lord's Supper.

As a young religious enthusiast, I expected I know not what manifestations of the Spirit, in fulfilling these ordinances. I fear I had a sense that in making such a great sacrifice, I should also have some return of special blessing—(a return which poor human nature always looks for, confessed or not)—but I was disappointed. I felt nothing, and was certainly determined not to pretend that I felt anything; so, while I observed that the men and women around me bowed their heads and covered their faces, I, hating the faintest shade of hypocrisy, sat bolt upright, listening to all and observing all, but by no means complacent with myself that I could feel no more. I was seeking religion in the outer form, rather than in the living spirit, which it takes years to learn and experience; and writing this to-day, after forty years have passed, I now regard ordinances with no more appreciation than a Quaker does, feeling that the sublime spirit of Christ's life should inspire more than a sentiment, should live in more than a ceremony, and that it should beget deeds like His, to renew, and purify, and inspire the world.

A few weeks after this, I went with a cousin to visit my mother's relations in Gloucestershire, probably determined on by the fact that I was then at liberty to do so, having, since I left my brother at the shop, no definite business occupation. My cousin was to be married, and when that event was over, I had to return to Cropredy. After visiting about for several weeks, the year was getting dark and sad. My uncle Thomas' large family of girls—there were ten of them, all at home—were looking forward to Christmas, and had already made me promise to stay till then. They were a happy household, living at Tetbury, a small market town in the west of Gloucestershire, where my uncle

Thomas, recently dead, had been established some years as a grocer and cheese factor. Treated with especial kindness by my aunt and elder cousins, and with mingled love and respect by the younger ones, who seemed to like me all the better for being so serious and silent, I was quite at home in this busy orderly home, where no servant was kept. My aunt, a handsome stately lady of few words and commanding presence, insisted that each should take her place and part in the domestic duties of the house.

A few weeks after, in the midst of our busy plans and purposes, I was surprised to receive a letter from my father, sent on from my last address, informing me that our minister and his wife were leaving the Cropredy neighbourhood. Being connected with the Baptist Home Missionary Society, he had been appointed to Brough in Westmorland. My cousins, seeing me crying as I read the letter, came round me with sad faces, asking what was the matter, expecting to hear some one was either ill or dead. When they found it was only the minister going away, girl like, they thought that was nothing, and protested I should stay as I had promised till after Christmas. But this was not to be.

I set off on my homeward journey on foot, and found myself silently following a tall boy, in a clean white smock frock, who was carrying my box. Gloucestershire is a lovely, picturesque county, and the afternoon was an exquisite one, being fine and dry and silent about the middle of November. Everywhere there was a sad melancholy breath of wind, at times, stirring among the leaves and hovering among the great branches by the roadside, as if to show how surpassing beautiful they were in their rich variegated autumnal dyes, and how re-splendently they decorated the peaceful earth.

So with sad and silent thoughts, my guide and I arrived at my cousin's, who had been in Oxford-shire with us. There he had learnt his trade, and there he had married his wife. Consequently I was received very kindly by both of them, and entertained very hospitably; but I fear I was a depressing guest. Having been apprised we should find my brother George at Chafford, my cousin drove me in his lumbering old gig —which most farmers kept in those ante-railway times—starting early on the Monday morning. Arriving there we found George, and were soon off again, pursuing our slow way over rough cross country roads, over hill and dale, and lessening the distance, as we constantly felt, between us and our journey's end. Young and strong as we were, we grew somewhat worn out and weary with our long day's travel and some of its less pleasant incidents —twelve hours and more in coming sixty miles, with only a stoppage of half-an-hour now and then, to bait the horse !

Getting a good night's rest at home, I was on foot early next morning, with my father, journeying to the residence of the minister, Mr. Osborn, two miles or more away. He was leaving that morning for Westmorland, and my visit was to be a last farewell, as I thought. We got there before day-light, and found busy preparations were being made for the minister's departure. It was arranged— with my father's consent—that I was to stay to keep Mrs. Osborn company, during her husband's absence.

Some time after preaching his trial sermons, he received a "call" to become minister of the church;

and then wrote to my father and myself suggesting that I might perhaps be willing to accompany his wife and baby to the north. This proposal came upon me with great surprise, as I had never once thought of such a thing. With our untravelled village ideas (before the opening up of the great central railways of the country), Westmorland was as far removed almost to the rustic "southron" intellect then, as Sydney is to-day. I remember a neighbouring farmer, in a white smock-frock, re-marked to my father, in broad Oxonian, that he had "heerd that 'twas a very mountaineous countree."

I soon became reconciled to the journey, and was delighted with the idea of seeing places of which I knew nothing but the name. But my father; how should I leave my father, whose love and tenderness I had never had reason to doubt? Under a calm countenance, he, on his part, hid a deeply troubled heart. For three nights, as mother told me, he could not sleep nor come to any decision. At last he consented that I might go and stay three months, and then return home. So I left Cropredy on these conditions, but I had a presentiment that I was going to return no more, which proved too true.

Well then, I was going to the north, and consequently all at once became an important personage, indeed, much more so than I wished to be. Everybody I met or saw had something to say or ask about it. Whoever had heard of this outlandish place, Westmorland, or had ever heard of or seen any one who had? But the weeks flew past, ending all this village talk, and much else beside.

The railway between York and Darlington had already been opened, and that also between Birmingham and the north; therefore, our plan was to travel to the latter place in a light van, under the care of my brother George, while Mrs. Osborn's furniture and luggage followed in another van. We left Oxfordshire on the 2nd of February, 1842, when I was within a few days of twenty years old. We were up very early that winter morning. But early as we had to start, we did not leave without observing the time-honoured rule of our home, namely, to have a word of prayer before parting; and, as my father used to say, put ourselves under the protection of Providence.

So that morning, our early breakfast over—the last thing before the horse was brought out—we stood there altogether, once more to sing a parting hymn, before our long and tedious journey commenced, into a country we knew nothing of, and unto a people we had as yet not seen. The broken strains of heavenly words entered our souls, and softened all our hearts. Solitary neighbours and cottage women, knowing that we were to start that morning, stood outside by the yet lighted window, all anxious to say a last good bye, and all mingling their own devout wishes for our good. There was quite a congregation when we rose from our knees; but there was little said. Our hearts were full.

The neighbours who had not yet got up to see us off, hearing the wheels turn on to the road, opened their chamber windows at which they stood, and called out their good byes and God bless yous to me. My father mounted me on our old pony, as he intended walking a few miles on the road. Eight miles he walked by my side that morning, drawn on partly by its bright pure air. Many a tender counsel was given, many a wise hint dropped. Dear father! he knew much more of the world than I did; and finally we parted.

We were soon at Birmingham, where my brother saw us all right for York, *en route* for Darlington. As it was a fine bright day, we were much taken up with viewing the beautiful country through which we passed. Being the first time I had seen or been in a railway carriage, I was not without some sense of the gravity of our position. I especially shuddered, and held fast by something, every time we cut through an arch, thinking the peculiar crashing noise very frightful; perhaps turning pale, as I remember a clerical looking gentleman, who rode in the same carriage, remarking to Mrs. Osborn about my seeming to be afraid.

But all went well. My fears were needless; and my experiences of railway travelling on that first day, were very pleasant. The one great difference between then and now being the small number of passengers travelling with the train, and the greater quietude of the stations. There were but single lines laid down then, and it all seemed such a private affair compared with the great bustling crowded centre of anxious and stirring people it is to-day. What autocrat ever conferred on the world such benefits and blessings, as the hero of Chatmoss, George Stephenson?

We reached Darlington about nine o'clock the same night, and thought it a special providence, that a quiet looking man came to the carriage door, and asked if we wanted lodgings. He offered to conduct us to his house, which we both (taking note of his honest countenance) readily accepted. We found his home very clean and comfortable, and his wife a bright cheerful woman, who soon got us a substantial tea after our long day's travel. In retiring to rest, what was our joy to hear the old familiar sounds of earnest prayer ascending from the ground-floor, where the family apparently knelt in devout worship, before retiring for the night. These sounds quieted every fear of evil, which our being in a strange place had tended to excite.

We had to start at eight o'clock in the morning by the coach for Barnard Castle, and thence to Brough. To our dismay, we found there were rival coaches running, one only of which went through to Brough. They both protested, speaking in a dialect of which we knew little or nothing, and we did not know which to believe. Our host, who had come up with us, pointed to the right one; but the other declared he was going also that day; took possession of our luggage, and crammed Mrs. Osborn and her baby inside the coach, there being no place for me, but on the top. Shouting defiant words to his rival, off we drove. I had little doubt afterwards the other driver was saying that I should be frozen to death, riding on the top of the coach over Stainmore on such a day, and that he would be guilty of my death. I believe this would have been the case in reality, had the man not pulled up at a roadside inn, and brought a glass of steaming brandy and water, and insisted on my drinking it right off.

The cold was something awful at that elevation for any human being to bear, much less a thinly clad, fragile woman from the south, unaccustomed to the northern temperature. The fact is, that when we got on to Stainmore, I seemed absolutely to have no clothing on, and the piercing winds blew through and through me with such rigour as to be quite terrific and appalling. I kept my seat, crowding head and knees together as best I could

for warmth ; and though at any other time I should
have refused the offer of brandy and water, I took
it eagerly, feeling that I must do so. When we got
to Barnard Castle, the people at the inn told us
how we had been misled. We went on to Brough
by the other coach, and I had the privilege of going
inside with my friends. My experience of riding
on the top of a coach over Stainmore, in the early
part of February, was never forgotten.

CHAPTER VI.

WE entered Brough by a long and slowly-descending road. It lies directly under mountains where are lead mines, which yield profit and employment to its inhabitants, whose chief occupation is mining. It is, or rather was—for it is now forty years ago— a long street of uncouth, white-washed, and many of them one storeyed houses. The largest and most handsome of these were the two posting houses, Macgee's and Kilvington's, with a few shops in the lower part, of very unpretending aspect, drapery being exhibited in one window and grocery in the other. The thrifty inhabitants thought it prudent apparently to ensure making the two ends meet, by being as comprehensive as possible.

There were converging rows of clean, comfortable looking houses, in some cases of superior appearance and pretensions, branching out from the principal street, and scattered far about. Smaller houses also everywhere, near the beck, ran parallel with the mountains we had crossed. The beck, a shallow yellow stream, flowed, as many of them do, from a great height, over a broken rocky bed, and rattled down with noisy clamour on stormy days. Church Brough, as its name denotes, is where the church and vicarage are; then a rather dismal, quiet place, at which a few old people only seemed to live; functionaries of the church and beadledom generally. In this remote place, with its rigorous climate and consequent poverty, dissent held the first and foremost rank; and the church, though a very handsome one, seemed to have been relegated to the background.

Our days of travel had been fine dry ones; the snow still lying thick and spotless on Stainmore, as it usually does all winter long, and even far into spring. Our friend who had preceded us thither, was at the coach door ready to receive us. But had we been Esquimaux, the curiosity of the younger part of the people in the street could hardly have been greater, so rudely did they press into our very midst, staring in our faces and watching our every movement. And what struck me on that, and many other occasions afterwards, was that they talked about us in our hearing—not only young people, but men and women also—as though they thought we should not know or understand what they said. I suppose it was because they could not understand us, which we found at first, on some occasions, they did not.

Mr. Osborn was staying *pro tem* with one of the most conspicuous men in the town, the mining agent, who was a Baptist. It was but a small house, with a window at the back, looking over the brawling, yellow beck. The entrance was by folding doors—with glass at the top, and brass knocker—opening in quite a stylish kind of way, into a rather broad lobby, which door gave persons on first entering, the impression of its being a much more commodious house than it really was. But among those primitive people, we soon found it was considered quite a genteel residence ; and we ourselves, coming from the thatched roofs of our native Oxfordshire, thought so, too, as it had to us the great merit of being slated.

The first night, our new house—notwithstanding our united efforts to reduce its chaos to something like makeshift comfort—came far short of our real needs and desires. One of the Baptist members, coming in and seeing our difficulty, suggested that I might sleep at his sister's, who was Squire Hobson's wife. It was at once decided to accept this kind offer, if confirmed; and our new friend sallied forth up street, to his sister's. He was soon back again, with a favourable answer.

Young and strong, and good sleeper though I then was, I was cold on going to bed, and cold I remained all the night through, counting every hour, till at length wearied out with wakefulness, I listened for the rising of the servant, which I expected would be about six o'clock or soon after. I determined that as soon as I heard her stirring, I would rise and ask her to let me out. The fact was, that we natives of the south were so imperfectly educated at that period, that we knew nothing of the differences of the climate we had to contend against. Inapprehensive of this fact, we were far too thinly clad for a journey to the north in midwinter.

Through this ignorance, I nearly lost my life; as we afterwards found that the winter dress of northern women differed materially from that worn

I. 6

by those of the south. In the old times, as I have heard it said, the women of the south wore the same clothing winter and summer, scorning to make any difference, lest they should be thought to want hardihood. Indeed, so far as knowledge went, we had been very badly equipped for our journey, none of the thousand springs of incidental hearsay, between the far north and the provincial south, being then in existence.

Consequently, for the first few weeks of our residence at Brough, we were in a most awkward predicament, quite as bad as though we had been in a foreign country; knowing nothing of the great difference in manners, habits, and modes of living of the inhabitants; nor yet understanding their grotesque dialect,—at least, to our ears it had a grotesque sound with it—while the common people of Brough seemed wholly inapprehensive of what we said. Thus on the first day after our arrival, wanting some additional furniture, Mr. and Mrs. Osborn went to Appleby to purchase it, leaving me and the baby at home, with a woman who lived in a cottage close by us, to clean and put things to rights.

Never shall I forget poor Betty's consternation

when I asked her to bring me different things, nor her puzzled looks to understand what I meant. The people of Brough used the same words for different vessels. A washing pan or bowl being a "pot," and a saucepan, a "pan" only; almost everything thus having a fresh name. When Betty failed to bring what I wanted, she stood with anxious face to see what the article was I brought when I went for it myself, smiling good naturedly, as I did, at her odd mistakes. Their's was, in fact, a more limited vocabulary than ours, as I found.

Thus the word "pots," though very unseemly to a southern woman's ears, was applied to all sorts of things made of "clay;" and Betty would ask, to my astonishment, if she should wash the "pots" and side them up, when she directed my attention to the china standing on the tray, after having been used at tea. In the same way she stroked the baby, and called it a "puir lal silly thing," and "an unco bonny barne," which, but for her kindly honest face, seemed very offensive terms. I had never before then heard of "barne," but in connection with a place with immense folding doors, used by farmers for storing and thrashing corn; nor "silly" but as meaning stupid or foolish. When I told them these dialect phrases at night, and said that I thought Betty meant it all in kindness, they laughed at our conversation, and said they were sure she did, though she had an odd way of expressing it.

During my early days at Brough, I often went into Betty's cottage on some trifling errand, and was shocked one evening to see her pouring out on a shallow platter, what I conceived to be "pigs' victuals" for her husband's supper, as he sat at the three-legged table on which the platter stood, with his mouth wide open to catch every word I said. Of course, I reported all at home, with many pitying words, sorry, as I said, that they were so very poor. The next time Betty came in, Mrs. Osborn asked her what that was which she made for her husband's supper. "That's poddish," says Betty. "They're good. Ivvery body sups them here. Oor Isaac's gey fond o' his poddish, but (pointing to me) this young lady quite flounders him. He can't mak oot what she says." At this we all laughed heartily. However, we soon learnt that porridge was *not* "pigs' victuals," although it looked very like it to my southern eyes.

We were long in getting into an easy apprehension
of the common talk of the people, and apparently,
they also of ours. Their loud emphatic tones
resembled those of talkers in a storm, who mean
patiently to say out all they have to say, notwithstanding the fury of the wind; which sounded to
our ears something very different from the soft
musical accent of the rapidly speaking Oxonians.
This rapidity of speech, I suspect, it was that hin-
dered the people generally from understanding us,
and talking of us before our faces as though we
were foreigners, which they did persistently for a
long time.

A butcher and his son argued the question,
whether Mrs. Osborn or myself was "t' mistress,"
in the presence of whichever of us happened to go
to order the meat, much to our amusement; the
old man always protesting that I was the mistress
of the house, as I was dark and serious looking;
and the son just as tenaciously holding that the
little fair one was "t' reet un."

But from the first, we were strongly impressed
with the genuine kindliness, honesty, and truthfulness of these people; their readiness to render us

any little service, or inform us of anything relating
to their customs, etc., they thought we did not
know; or do anything, indeed, they could to oblige.
There was no trace, it is true, of southern syco-
phancy, so offensive and humiliating in the village
peasantry of the midland counties; no timid
curtsying of the women and girls, nor speechless
bowing and bare-headed reverence of the men and
boys to superiors. They were a race of hardy,
thrifty toilers; and neither bishop, nor priest, nor
squire exerted any arbitrary personal power over
them; and this they showed in their personal
independence and freedom, as you continually felt.

But as a set off to their bluntness, and apparent
want of courtesy, you met with no make belief, and
hypocrisy was almost unknown, as were its twin
vices, sham and cant, the outgrowths too often of
our older civilizations.   As a result of this, we soon
began to like these honest, hardy people, and to
appreciate and prefer their superior energy in character and action, to the more effeminate southern
whom we had left. These northerners we soon
found were more resolute, energetic, daring, and
courageous; willing to learn to an amazing degree,

so long as what you wanted to teach them accorded with these characteristics. They took nothing on trust. But they were not great talkers: whoever knew great workers to be so?

The Baptists and religious people among whom we principally moved, were silent to a singular degree; both silent and shy. Some ladies, who owned considerable property, and lived on their own estate, being so shy that they rarely lifted their eyes however long they talked to you, nor even if they called on you; and yet they were fair, handsome, unmarried women. There were many of the most devout and pious of the Baptist women, beside them, who had this singular manner, reminding one of the devout women of the early Christian ages, when they foreswore the secular intercourse of earth for the holier intercourse of heaven.

The men also were shy and silent, though not to the same degree, but often quite painfully so. I have heard a young student, who was once with us, say, that in coming back from his round of this circuit, he invariably met one of the members, who was a farmer, at a certain point, and all that ever he said was, "Travelling home again, are you?"

—every time just the same, and no more—though he often stopped at the man's house to bait his pony, as he passed it on the road.

In fact, we soon found we had come among a singularly original people, of unquestionable sincerity and an inflexible uprightness of purpose, and of an unusual loftiness of religious aim and action. Hence I was much invigorated and stimulated by their intercourse, and their strong faith and religious energy quickened and strengthened mine also. In all things there was less talk than deed, and by nothing that was done did they ever create the impression that they wanted to attract attention to themselves. Their temporal privations and many hardships, their personal toil amid endless disappointments, their cultivation and care bringing no increase—or an increase too tardy to be of any avail—such, for instance, as their never-ripening crops, or their crops being rendered unfit to bring to the barn door through inclement weather. These and other perplexing trials had done more to chasten and reconcile them to their fate, than ever the asceticism of the anchorite, or the austeri-

ties of the old world monks had done for the truth
and beauty of religion.

No people I had then, or have since met with,
have impressed me with having a religion so true
and pure and lofty as theirs. To me, who had
only recently given up the world, and vowed to live
apart from all its ensnaring fascinations, and who
had, like themselves, felt something of the difficulties and disappointments of life, they were especially
interesting and soul-inspiring.

But to revert to my own more personal experience. I now began to feel that I had lost my own
dear home, the love and sympathy of my own dear
father, and that I was a stranger in a strange land.
The attention I had formerly received, when a
visitor for a few days only with my friends, gradually falling off, and altogether declining into nility
or sometimes positive coldness. This, I have no
doubt, my father feared, and it was probably the
real cause of his objection to my going; not that
he had any fear of my making myself a useful and
valuable help to them. He knew my self-sacrificing
spirit, and that I would eat no man's bread without
fully earning it; but he also knew how poor the

people were that my friends were going amongst, and how small a salary the minister consequently would have.

However, the members of the church soon seemed fully apprehensive of my situation and its unpleasantness; and in proportion as they saw me becoming anxious and troubled, manifested great interest in me, and showed me much kindness; not without increasing the very evils, perhaps, which they, in consideration of my comfort, wished to diminish. But in all that related to myself, I was making no sort of revelations to any one, not even consulting with my father by letter, as I perhaps ought to have done.

There was this at the bottom of it. I was now very anxious, and thought it my duty, being twenty years of age, to relieve my father altogether for the future of any care on my account. I hoped every day, perhaps foolishly, that something would occur to afford me a chance of getting a situation. I had had a presentiment all along, that I was to stay in the north, and now I had become so prepossessed with the lofty religious aspirations of these people, which was the primary object of my life, that I longed to remain among them.

Happily money with me, only in so far as I really needed it for necessary articles of clothing, was not coveted then, as many other things were; although pressing needs in this direction, at times, made me very sad. I sent no word, nor made any complaint to any one, not even to my father, from whom I thought it right to hide all my sorrows, showing him the bright side only when I wrote, knowing what a troubled, struggling life he had had for many years. No, he should never know how anxious and unhappy I was at times; nor would I send to him for money, for had he not long before paid my expenses to the north? And now I would struggle hard to provide for myself.

So I set to work after I went to bed at night, in the attic in which I slept, to repair and alter the things I had, to the best of my ability, making myself a dress out of a silk cloak I wore on Sundays, as I very well remember. Many a night, I was thus employed till one or two o'clock in the morning, only giving over when I could keep myself awake no longer. Yet I was punctually up and down again at the usual hour, having the little ones with me, and everything ready for breakfast. They knew nothing of my extra midnight labours, nor were at all apprehensive, I suppose, of my sad reflections. But the spiritual discipline I gained from it was great, and like the experience of the saints of the middle ages, I felt myself continually growing calmer and stronger under it.

On this account it was, I believe, that so much attention and respect was shown me on all occasions, by these deeply religious people, who instinctively seemed to apprehend all my inner secrets, and discern the meaning of my most private ideas. They held that *all* should use their "gifts," as they called it, at the prayer meetings, which we found they did, women as well as men engaging in oral prayer. Mr. Osborn insisted that his wife and I should overcome our timidity, and do as the other members did ; and one night at family worship he got me to venture upon this untried duty. From that time, he and others frequently called upon me, and my confidence grew stronger every time. All winter through they had the prayer meetings at the members' houses in rotation, and very pleasant they were, a large bright fire being made up in the best room for the occasion.

During the summer months, when agricultural pursuits kept many members in the fields, if not all, the meetings were held in the chapel. Then the attendance was very scant, for these people believed in being faithful in all things. At such times, I have seen only myself and the doorkeeper present. The doorkeeper was named Joseph, a man of original character. He heeded not numbers, and either gave out a hymn he knew, or asked me to read one.

I saw much of Joseph, and felt as a child in the presence of a good father. I attended many a prayer meeting with him alone in the chapel there. His striking prayer—as though in reality talking to a loving parent, on whom he relied for help and hope in all his troubles—was a great blessing to me. He also encouraged me to pray, which I did on several occasions. I have never forgotten the quiet benediction which fell on my anxious heart, as he bade me good-night at the chapel door, saying meekly: "Bless the Lord! We have had a good time to-night." Much of my capability to speak and lecture in public in after years, I derived from using my "gifts," as these good people called it, at the week-night prayer meetings, at Brough, in Westmorland.

I also read a few highly instructive and, to me, deeply interesting books while there. Dr. Thomas Brown's "Moral Philosophy," and the "Elements of Mental Science," by some Scotch metaphysician whom I cannot now name, though it made a deep impression on my mind at the time; also Whately's "Logic," and others. I should say here, perhaps, that at this period, if not before, I always made a point of making the contents of every book I read my own. I had not time to take notes, nor did I do so, but every page I read I earnestly endeavoured to make myself sure of understanding. This method of reading I found to be the best, as the act of taking notes diverts, in some degree, the mind from the subject.

There was one more book about this time, or later in the same period, that made a profound impression on my mind, the author of which indeed became a great master, and was one of the moulders of my life. This was Emerson, the American essayist. I was doing the usual morning dusting in the room which my friend used for his study, when I caught sight of an open pamphlet. I stopped my work for a moment to look at it. I found it was the essay on Nature, lying open at the Christian Teacher, I stopped to read the paragraph on the Snow Storm. It was all I dare read. It woke in my soul a thousand new and wonderful thoughts. I could not forget it. I was so ravished with the genial freshness and fertility of its argument, and the rare spiritual unction flowing through it, that whenever I could get a chance I read it over and over again, till I knew it by heart as I knew the Psalms of David or some of my favourite hymns.

Spiritual life I now saw was a fertile source of intellectual vigour, as I have ever since found; and that the highest capacities of the soul interact that "intellect is always holy: holiness always wise." It was, in fact, a new spirit world, a mysticism, on whose border I had been long walking and dreaming with indefinable fancies. I felt that I had affinities with the highest in nature, and that all heights of being and character were within my reach and attainment.

CHAPTER VII.

My first school was at Brough in Westmorland. While I had been working very hard in the minister's family, without either pay or thanks, for many months, I was beginning to feel that after all I should have to give up this vague waiting and hoping, and reluctantly make up my mind to go home again. When all at once (as though all the thoughts of my inner heart had been known), I was asked by several of the female members of the church, whether I would teach a girls' school, in case they could get a sufficient number of pupils.

At that time, there was not a girls' school either in Brough or the neighbourhood. The only school then in the small market town, being a private school for boys, kept by an aged Independent minister, in his own small cottage.

I was very shy and diffident, and pleaded inability and want of training, etc. To these objections they put forth that the girls were either very young or backward, through having had no "mistress" there, as they termed it, for a long time. There was, of course, much discussion on the subject; and I found that everybody, even the minister and his wife, when it came to the point of my returning home, wanted to keep me in the north. Notwithstanding my shyness and reserve, I soon felt I had found great favour among these primitive people. There were strong affinities between us, not only spiritual but temporal. Faithful in all heavenly duties, their religion included a due sense of faithfulness in every service unto mankind.

A tolerably large house chanced to be standing empty at the upper or quieter end of the town; and part of this house was taken for the use of a school room, etc. I rode over to Appleby one evening, on Mr. Osborn's pony, to get a few circulars printed by a man named Barnes, who kept a humble shop there (neither printer nor bookseller existing in Brough at that time). I began my little school the following week. It seemed at first a very unpromising affair, ruinous to my air castles mostly, and trying to me in many other ways. I had got rooms, but was entirely destitute of anything to put in them. My upper room, where I was to live, being as bare as ever was saint's cell, without the saint's contentment and resignation.

Very small at first, my school gradually increased. As I became better known, I had often grown up girls whose education had been neglected. These mostly came from lone farm houses, and were sometimes as tall as myself. Blithe, sonsie lasses they were for the most part, willing and obedient, and rendering me an amount of respect which I seemed almost ashamed to take. I may say that my grammar at that time was like that of country ladies generally, very superficial; though in after life it became one of my favourite studies.

The people of Brough at that time were not rich. Mining and agriculture engaged the attention, and in some cases divided the occupation of the people.

In consideration of this, I had been advised—as my own conscience would have dictated—to make my charges very low. Though I eventually got a considerable number of pupils together, they did ittle more than pay needful expenses; and in the early days of my little enterprise, I was often reduced to the most straitened circumstances.

Once, I remember, I had not a single penny left to buy the least needful article of food, and was in sad inward trouble as to what I should do. I tried to settle the question, whether I should fast till some one brought me some money, or ask Mrs. Osborn to lend me a shilling.

I had never before asked for such favour, and I reflected that she might not have one, or, if she had, might not be able to spare it. It was Saturday. I had no school, and was going down the street to my friends' house on some errand—sad enough—when one of my pupils came up to me and said her mother had sent her to pay the shilling she owed me. I need not say how my heart leaped up in silent but devout gratitude to God for his goodness that day, for I sincerely believed then, as I do now, that it came from Him.

I helped myself by thus holding on. From the first day of my leaving home I vowed that whatever I had to suffer, I would try by all the means in my power to keep myself from going back to the old village life, where there was neither help nor hope for a person of intellectual aspirations. Very hard work and hard fare, week after week, and month after month, such as I submitted to, was very depressing, with no happy outlook of any kind beyond it. No congratulatory eyes met mine then, as in the old time, when I walked beside my dear father, and felt in his quiet smiles both sympathy and encouragement.

Coming from the south of England, as I did, where Nature's pictures, like those of the kaleidoscope, were beautiful still, through all her many changes and seasons, filling the soul with impressioned dreams of radiant greenery and sylvan loveliness—I never could like Brough, or reconcile myself to that long dreary prospect of snow-covered fells, which for more than half the year encompassed it all around. Its inhospitable, ungenerous skies, as I still thought them, never won me over to delight, or kept my heart from sighing for a kinder and brighter home. It was not a place to love, nor to add to one's happiness. We all felt it was only probationary, and held our peace. A morrow would come, and for that morrow we lived. That was a recognised fact on all hands.

With this feeling we got through our time, till the third year, when an incident occurred in my apparently sad life, which might have had happier results, with a less conscientious person. I state it merely as an indication of my feelings respecting marriage, which ordinance is now subverted to such vile uses and abuses—women, in reality, being bought and sold in the marriage market as in any other.

One fine Sunday in summer, a young man, who —as the preacher appointed for the day at Brough— came to dine with Mrs. Osborn after morning service, in the absence of her husband. I also was there, quiet and retiring as usual, not presuming to say scarcely a word, though I sat at the same table. The young man was shy and silent. He was above the middle stature, and having a deformed foot, he walked with arms continually hanging down by his sides, as if to balance himself.

A woman was to preach at the Primitive Methodist chapel in the afternoon, and some of the young people of the Baptist congregation had arranged to go, and promised to call for me. Mr. J—— on hearing where we were going, was interested, and said he would go too. We formed quite a company. On coming back, the merits of

the sermon were rather warmly discussed, so much
so that the majority of the company sped on forgetting that they were leaving Mr. J—— behind.
As he was Mrs. Osborn's guest, I thought it my
duty to wait, and walk by him. This I did as my
duty, talking to him in a friendly manner all the
way we went, for we were left far behind. It is
true I felt some reserve in doing this, knowing that
he was rich, and, in certain respects, my superior.

I went to my school as usual, on the Monday
morning. It had grown larger. Many older girls
came from several villages round about; and the
teaching of some thirty pupils occupied all my time
and thoughts. Much to my surprise, on Tuesday
afternoon, Mrs. Osborn sent me word that I was
wanted very particularly, and must come at once.
I set my school free, and then went down to her
house. She met me much more graciously than
usual, saying, it seemed I had captured Mr. J——
on Sunday. I thought—though we were the most
realistic of people—that she was joking; and
persisted gravely that I was innocent of any intention of doing such a thing. Then she told me
he had confessed all to her, saying, "It is you he

has come to see, and no one else"—and added, " you had better not be too hard with him : he is so very shy."

There was, perhaps, some need of saying this, as she knew how likely I would be to keep him at a distance, as I did other young men. As a consequence of her information, I refused to go down stairs till she was ready, so that she might do all the talking, as usual. Mr. J—— was an eccentric man for his age, never having had any need to work, and, owing to his deformed foot, hardly capable of it. For this reason, and his delicate health, he had been spoiled as a child.

An elder brother and he lived together on a large farm ; and Mr. J—— rode about on a good horse, wherever he went, on account of his lameness. Being a man of thirty, and having his own will and way in everything, you may imagine something of what he was; the quiet smile on his face being, to a woman, the one redeeming feature in the *tout ensemble.*

As religious people in a religious home, we took tea very pleasantly together, but very quietly. I for my part talked a little more than usual. The gentleman at length left to get his horse ready for home, without making his wishes known to me himself. It is probable, knowing I had no relations there, he had spoken to Mrs. Osborn, expecting that she would help him by introducing the subject, but she did neither. However, as one blessed result, I was treated with more consideration by my friends, and the additional kindness was exceedingly welcome and consoling to me.

I was back at my school on the morrow after this event, a little graver and more commanding, as well as more absolute. The thought of having been loved, always gives a woman new strength. This little episode in my dull life at Brough, if it did nothing else, made it somewhat pleasanter. It showed possibilities—such possibilities being that I might not remain a second Cinderella always. I was now spoken to as an equal, and in some degree allowed to take the liberties of one. The rude hints I had often had to bear, from that time ceased. Mrs. Osborn had herself heard the story, and knew its truth.

A prospect of change came about this time. Mr. Osborn had been sent to Carlisle to preach a trial sermon; and a few months after he was appointed to go there. This change was looked forward to with great gladness. For various reasons, my friends pressed me to go with them, knowing that I, like themselves, had not been happy where we were, nor had my school ever paid me. With the utmost thrift I had, indeed, lived on the hardest fare—brown bread being my continual diet, and a bit of butter now and then my only relish.

My father was against my remaining at Brough alone, so I at once decided to give up my school and go. When all my little bills were paid me, I found I had a few pounds left, as I had contracted no debts. Out of this money I bought some necessary articles of plain and comfortable clothing, and thought myself very rich to be able to do so. I had, moreover, five pounds left, over and above, which my friends perceiving, made a point of borrowing. In those days I did not need much pressing. The fact that they were greatly in need, and that I could supply that need, became a veritable certainty that I should do so.

CHAPTER VIII.

WE started for Carlisle in Squire Hobson's phaeton, by which mode we rode to Penrith. From there we took the coach to Carlisle, now more than forty years ago, on a late autumn day, when the roads were sloppy with rain, and the dykes choked with a variegated compound of scattered leaves.

We entered the old Border city rather late in the afternoon, and landed with the mail coach at the "Crown and Mitre," in Castle-street. Few people were astir, and the city presented a very uncompromising aspect. We stayed in Castle-street over night, and in the morning went down to William-street, Botchergate, where we had a comfortable double house taken.

Mr. Osborn preached for the Baptists for four or five years, at the Athenæum, in Lowther-street (now the Post Office), at the end of which time, the Baptist Home Missionary Society, hearing that he had become heterodox, ceased to pay.

There was plenty of employment for me in this new home, where everything had to be adjusted afresh, and a whole house put into order, with seven souls to provide for—father and mother, three babies, a young student, and myself. But after the first week or two, things dropped into their places, and the old use and wont was pretty much established.

The Baptists at first were almost our sole visitors; but what little we saw of the city interested us much. It was above all so very untown-like; many of the people so quaint, quiet, and slow; and hardly any of them habitually bright, or brisk, or stately, or with an air of superior intelligence, or breeding; and none of them had that portly pomposity continually to be met with among the wealthy citizens of the south, or even among the village squires and freeholders. The rapid speech, quick motions, and sharp physique, with the distinct *esprit de corps* of the market town of any size in the south, were entirely wanting here, or at least it seemed so then.

They were tradesmen, money makers, very possibly rich, but they had neither the manners nor the deportment of gentlemen; and the same deficiency

was seen everywhere in the gentler sex also. Almost
anyone coming from the south, forty years ago,
would, I think, have been of the same opinion;
and would have noted the absolute want of genuine
polish and politeness. I fancy this arose from
the large lordly heritages of the southern gentry,
squires, and farmers, who were mostly all large
freeholders, and in nearly every particular different
from the northern farmer. The southern farmers
were men of wealth. They sat in their parlours,
and were waited upon by servants. They knew
little or nothing of farm work, and their children
were educated by governesses, and sent to the best
boarding schools. Of course, they had been bred
gentlemen for generations; hence the difference
between north and south; especially the difference
between northern and southern towns half a century
ago.

The northern man, as a compensation, possessed
a richer and more fertile brain, a readier hand, a
stouter heart, and a courage to win kingdoms;
never a gentleman; and yet it is noteworthy that
many of them possessed true nobility of purpose,
which had become a birthright to them through

the bold and enduring conquests of a long chain of ancestors. So Carlisle was an entirely new world to me, full of interest, it is true, but provoking a world of thought; and to a stranger, making every-thing seen or heard an object of quiet reflection and observation.

Carlisle improved on acquaintance. We found we had come among a shrewd, ready-witted, and dexterous people. We no sooner began to know them, than we began to respect them. A self-helpful, thrifty, and courageous people, I found in them the very qualities and sturdy virtues I most admired; along with the sterling honesty, truthfulness, and independence of the people of Westmorland; though with much less of their silent, lofty, and fervid piety. This peculiarity of the latter was owing to a great extent, no doubt, to their seclusion, loneliness and privations, which intensified and strengthened their ideas; hence arises, perhaps, the lofty patriotism—a kind of religion of the people —of mountainous countries.

The people of Carlisle excited my interest greatly on every hand, by ignoring the amenities of society, and following uncouth customs of their own, apparently much preferred on account of old and dear associations. Hence they carefully preserve these customs, and their dialect everywhere survives the Board School. The Lancaster and Carlisle Railway was opened soon after our coming to the city, as well as other lines, which have done so much to develope and brighten it, as well as to extend its boundaries. It has also mitigated the asperities of the old city. The railway has materially developed the life of cities and towns everywhere, making fifty years of the present equal in many things to a cycle of the past.

On coming into Carlisle, as a Baptist minister of more than average abilities, Mr. Osborn attracted many friends. His personal appearance, tall figure, and steep piled up forehead, were everywhere notice-able; added to which he was a voracious reader, mostly of theology and philosophy. Logic and grammar he had taken up at first, with a view to his own mental improvement.

Originally an Oxfordshire farmer's son, of the poorest kind, he had received none but the very simplest elements of education. To write a good hand sixty years ago, was in rural England in the

south, the top of the village schoolmaster's ambition
to teach, and of his rustic pupils' ambition to learn.
To read and write was the summary of the education
then given to poor boys in parish schools, and in
many villages there was no other.

Mr. Osborn was an excellent penman, but little
more ; hence, I suppose, he became a traveller for
a grocery establishment, at a later period of his life,
in which position he was when he first joined the
ministry.   He had first rate abilities as a thinker,
and was rather a bold reasoner, preferring abstruse
studies in metaphysics, mental science, and philosophical research generally, to history or literature.

He had, in fact, naturally a fine mind, but was
placed in the position of thousands of poor English
youths, without the means to obtain, or the time to
acquire, the necessary education to develope it.
So, like his class, he delighted to discuss deep
philosophical or metaphysical questions, books, and
intellectual topics, which he did with an unwearying
interest.

As to his piety, at the time of his coming into
Carlisle, it was deep and undoubted.   I have heard
him frequently close his studies at two o'clock in

the morning, in a small attic room, over the one in which I slept at their house at Brough, with an audible prayer of great depth and power, which he thought no one heard but God alone. Dissenting ministers of forty or fifty years ago, with considerable families, had often no more than seventy or eighty pounds a year as stipend, which was in reality the case with my friend.

Personally, in coming into Carlisle, I concluded to stay awhile with my friends. My help was greatly needed, though I knew they could not afford to pay me, nor even then to re-fund what they had borrowed. The expense of removing, with their limited finances, had exhausted all their resources. This threw me back into the same sad state of poverty as before. After buying a few needful articles of dress, I had lent them very nearly all I had; a half-crown, and two or three sixpences, alone remaining in my pocket. I soon saw that no word was ever said in extenuation of my poverty; no one suspected what I had done; nor did their behaviour to me as time ran on, tend to show that they were under obligation to me; but rather the reverse.

So I remember, one winter afternoon, I had been into my own room to change my dress, and before coming out, took up a pair of boots to put on. Before doing so, I examined the soles. Alas! they presented a sad sight to one who had no money in her pocket. They were worn out far beyond my thought or expectation. What should I do?

The fact is, I had once over acted indiscreetly. I had walked with the baby in my arms, often during the gloomy winter mornings, a short way from the end of William-street, my object being to pause awhile before the window of a small bookseller, named Fishburn. This I did to read over the titles of his books, and see if there was anything new. It amused baby to see the pictures as well as myself. One morning I was attracted by a rather thick faded copy of a book, the title page of which was open. It was lectures to the students of a French college by the lady principal. This arrested my attention, and excited my longing to read it. But how could I get hold of the book?

Mr. Osborn and his young student got books of old "Fish," as they called him, and said they could not do without them. I had the half-crown in my

I. 8

pocket—though I had offered it toward a subscription at the chapel, poor as I was—but to this offer they had wisely said "No." So at last, baby and I actually ventured to open the door, and ask the placid old man the price of the book in the window. He looked considerably surprised to see a plainly dressed young woman, with a baby in her arms, enquiring the price of such a book. But when he said half-a-crown, and I drew the money out of my pocket, he looked much more surprised.

Once I remember, during winter I bought a little worsted, and knit me a pair of hose, after going to bed at eleven o'clock at night: and as they objected to my having a light, I did the best I could, drawing the blind up to catch whatever light I could from the street lamp, happily not very far from my window.

I found an agreeable, well educated, and well mannered young lady among the Baptists. Her mother, who was the owner of considerable property in Botchergate, was a Mrs. Cummins, who lived there with her three daughters. This Miss Cummins was the youngest—light, fragile, and pretty. She wore glasses, and afterwards became the wife of Mr. J. A. Cockburn of Allenwood, near Carlisle. She offered to show me the sights of the old city, whenever I could find time to go and see them. So earnest was she, that she often prevailed upon Mrs. Osborn to let me off, when I would have been too proud to have asked her myself.

In this way, she took me to see many curiosities, so called, among which was the museum, then in a back room of the old Athenæum, shut up in disorder, and covered with dust. She was the nearest specimen of a southern lady I had seen in the north; bright, intelligent, and dressy. She seemed to be well acquainted with almost everything, from the Indian idol down to the pair of wee Chinese slippers. That awful couple of New Zealanders, which afterwards sent such a shudder through my frame in Finkle-street, was not there then.

More than an hour we spent together in the museum, that winter afternoon, examining and commenting on the various curiosities. Miss Cummins was a capital cicerone, and as I had an immeasurable faculty for listening, we both enjoyed the thing. From that day I never quite forgot the dusty old museum, nor ceased to wonder why in a place like Carlisle, so destitute of attractions, it was not brightened up, and put to some better use. Hence when the question of its preservation cropped up in the Corporation more than twenty years after, I knew some little of its past history, and was able to write on behalf of its preservation and being made the nucleus of a future museum. This, thanks to a few active minded men—headed by Mr. John Sinclair, afterwards its devoted secretary—was at length done, and the little museum was located in Finkle-street.

It is needless to mention other places which Miss Cummins took me to see; suffice it to say I was very anxious to see an assize trial. The scene was highly instructive and amusing to me. We had heard many romantic accounts in the south of Gretna Green marriages, and I had read a good deal about them in novels. What was my surprise then to find a real Gretna Green trial going on, and the old "blacksmith" and his helpful spouse there in person, with their veritable book in hand. The young man in the dock—a Cumberland lad of twenty-two, I think—he did not look so much— was undergoing trial for having been twice married at Gretna. Poor fellow! he was found guilty, and sentenced accordingly, the victim of unwise and thoughtless laws. That young man's serious face looks at me still through the many years in sad remonstrance.

But what made this trial doubly interesting to me, was that it occurred just after the elopement of Lady Clementeus Villiers. The whole batch of barristers —from the south, probably—were anxious, on that account, to get hold of the old man's book, and find her name in it. This they did, upon which there was such laughing among them, and such passing the book about, and pointing to it, as to quite bewilder the old priest. To me the Villiers case was interesting. The family had a seat at Upton Edgehills, their principal residence, within six miles of my home in Oxfordshire, which I had seen, and from which she had eloped.

There was one more case at the assizes—perhaps the saddest of all—that of a poor woman, who had taken her illegitimate boy out of the workhouse, presumably for a holiday. Instead of this, however, she had taken him three or four miles into the country, near to a lonely pond of water, in which he was afterwards found drowned. This was a long heart-rending case—hanging or nothing—and as no one had seen her do it—miserable creature!—she finally got off.

There was one more notable place I saw for the first time, in the company of my friend, Miss Cummins, and that was Corby woods. It was a lovely day; bud and blossom everywhere, the sky radiant with sunshine, the air balmy and soft, and not too hot. There were no strollers but ourselves, which to a reflective mind like my own, was a great point in the enjoyment. With all due respect to humanity, crowds always seemed to me to profane and desecrate nature, with their loud talk and flippant manners.

CHAPTER IX.

THERE were many things highly interesting to me while staying in William-street. The Baptists, who constantly came there, treated me very kindly and respectfully: and some of them, who knew I had had a school at Brough, tried to induce me to begin one in Carlisle. This I demurred to, preferring to wait. I had no means to do so properly, and was ambitious of more education. I felt I would rather stay a few months where I was, getting knowledge by reading, and hearing intellectual conversations and discussions without end.

Among the visitors was Mr. J. A. Cockburn, afterwards of Allenwood paper mill. He was then a member of the Baptist church; a great reader, especially of Carlyle, a keen politician, an animated talker, and a very gentlemanly man.

James Milligan was then among the Baptists, a young married man, a weaver, living at Trinity-buildings. He had a well-stored mind, and had been a great reader of the best literature; but, unfortunately, had an impediment in his speech. He wrote elegant verses and interesting letters. Two or three years later, at my suggestion—for we had become very intimate, through my verse making propensity—he gathered up the best of his poems, which had appeared in Whitridge's *Miscellany*. Some of these, especially "Sunset" and "Daybreak," struck me as being strikingly beautiful. They were issued in shilling pamphlet form by Mr. Whitridge. By this means the poor weaver realized sufficient funds to take him to America. In the New World, a doctor cured him of his stammering. Soon after he rose to be the editor of a newspaper, and lived to become a prosperous and much respected man.

Another man, who has since greatly distinguished himself, was the Rev. W. J. Tweddle, the son of a house-painter in Carlisle, then a student at the Wesleyan college at Didsbury. He called upon us occasionally when at home, and was always a genial and interesting friend, who could tell a lively and diverting story. As a preacher he has been long conspicuous for his pulpit eloquence in London and other large centres of population. His mind was one of clear and vivid perception, showing patient and careful thought. He had the penetration to see through the sophisms of an argument you wished to hide, and was capable of giving illustrations in beautiful diction and poetic language.

Many others came beside, whose object was more especially theology; young ministers and students, who got to know when Mr. Osborn was at home, for he then had good congregations at the Athenæum.

I was full of occupation during these months, and occasionally very grave and sad, as the fact of the necessity for my further efforts to help myself pressed more continually on my mind. But as I was situated, thank heaven, there was much to interest me. One day, the young student who stayed with Mr. Osborn, knowing me to be able to give an opinion, brought a copy of verses, which he said he was going to send to the *Carlisle Journal*. He told me the eldest Miss Cummins wrote verses, and that at her instigation he had tried his hand, and was very anxious that she should have an opportunity of seeing them in print. Mr. R. had by no means a brilliant intellect, nor any large measure of knowledge or reading, and Miss C. was of the same type. He read them. I remonstrated, telling him they would be rejected, as I saw they wanted reason as well as rhyme. But the vanity of the young minister prevailed, and the result was a well deserved humbling. Having allowed his verses to be seen and talked about, they were the cause of much laughter and amusement in our circle. I said nothing, but I thought I could write better, as I had written verses when younger, in imitation of uncle Newth's rhyming letters.

Mr. Osborn used to rally me and say, when none but his own family were present, that I was like none of the other young females—that I set my cap at none of the young men, nor cared for anybody whatever—which I felt was perfectly true, though a secret to myself alone. Had I been a duke's daughter, I could not have been more careful of keeping clear of any matrimonial liason than I was. I did not want matrimony; it was congenial labour I wanted. For this I prayed, and waited, and suffered. I often thought that my plainness and poverty were my best safe-guard. Moreover,

I was so grave and lofty—lived upon a mountain, as Mr. Osborn told me—that none of the opposite sex presumed to speak lightly to me.

But one thing is eternally true. Misfortunes and sorrows bravely borne come to an end, and hopes kept bright by the breath of prayer always prosper in the long run. The summer had come and gone, and a great part of the winter, too, and I was still working hard for nothing. My pocket was empty, and my heart sadly sorrowful, the perception of which displeased my friends, who got impatient with me, thinking, perhaps rightly, that I ought to be cheerful however troubled I might be.

At last a very slight event brought about a change in my life. I was blamed unjustly, wrongfully. This I could not bear. For all I had done, I had received no acknowledgment whatever; sometimes quite the reverse—was made to feel, though no words were said, that I was dependent on the Osborns. This I felt they knew to be untrue, or would, at least, when I was gone. This event had roused me to action; for I was proud, and though poor, of a very independent spirit. So I cried and prayed all the night through, but rose

in the morning to my work as usual, with a full
determination on action. I could not possibly stay
any longer, where I had been made to feel I was
no longer wanted.

I wrote out an advertisement for a preparatory
governess' situation. Before going with it to the
Journal office, I told Mr. Osborn calmly all that I
proposed doing. I showed him the paper, but he
said nothing either for or against it. It was about
the beginning of the year. I waited and waited,
but no application came, save one in the shape of a
cruel hoax.

However, in about a fortnight, when I was engaged with the work of the family, two ladies called,
wishing to see me with a view to an engagement.
They were from Scotby : Mr. Sutton's mother and
his wife's sister. I was not presentable then, but
went over in the afternoon. I saw Mrs. Sutton,
and was at once engaged. I entered on my new
duties at Candlemas. No youth or maiden of
Scripture times or sacred story being more surely
led by God than was I; or, I may say, no one
more clearly recognised the providential hand of
God leading me in the narrow path than I did.

I had but two or three days to prepare for my new situation, and they were very busy ones. First of all, I had to ask Mr. Osborn for another sovereign. I found if I asked for more it would be inconvenient for them. I had already had one out of the five which I had lent—this, with the new demand, left three unpaid. But my very scanty wardrobe, thanks to my persistent industry, was all ready in time; and with a feeling that I could brave being thought worse off than I really was, I entered upon the duties of my new home, among new and scrutinizing eyes.

CHAPTER X.

SCOTBY is a nice and pleasant village, a short distance from Carlisle, of which Mr. Sutton's leather works were—and still are—the central life and sole industry. The tanyard and working-men's dwelling houses, and the reading room, near the station, being the first objects of interest to attract the attention of strangers. It is a very clean and flourishing place. Mr. Sutton's residence stands in the centre of the village, in the midst of its own grounds, just beyond the modest Friends' meeting house and burial ground.

I found my new home eminently one of peace, order, and good manners; industry, thrift, and genial good sense, made the days go round with what at first appeared to be monotonous quietness, after my being used to the fuller and freer life of intellectual intercourse and aspirations. But as the spring advanced, and we were able to get out into the gardens and fields, I became more in love with the place, and likewise began to think more highly of its inhabitants. It is almost needless to say I had come into a veritable Quaker's family. The order, precision, and punctuality of the house, were for the first few weeks very oppressive. It was well for me that there were babies to engage my attention.

I got on very well, as my employment threw me a good deal into the society of Mrs. Sutton, whom I found an exceedingly well educated and well read lady, capable of talking on many, if not on all kinds of subjects. I had been careful at our first interview rather to underrate than overrate my own parts, telling her next to nothing about myself; not even that I had had a school, which she did not know till long afterwards. I was grave and circumspect, answering her numerous questions with regard more to their truth than my own honour, saying little more beyond than that I came from the south, which pleased her on account of my manner of speaking. Hence, for the first few months, she was constantly making discoveries in my favour.

I was then well read in Emerson, and had imbibed much of his Spartan spirit, which made me think very little of many of the Quaker proclivities, though

I admired very much their great religious principles, and their sterling nonconformity. Mrs. Sutton was surprised to find in her talks with me how much I knew of the history and principles of the Quakers, especially that I had read Jonathan Dymond's Essays, then a comparatively new book. She soon found my reading of books meant real knowledge. Yea, in one case, I had gone beyond her, and had read William Penn's "Sandy Foundation Shaken." This, she said, she had neither seen nor knew any one else who had.

But here let me say, that I was first of all careful and anxious to perform the duties of my situation, with care and exactness, and in a proper spirit. I was shrewd enough to know (as every young person should know), that whatever incidents of knowledge or reading I might display, would rather tell against than for me. In a word, I knew my conduct would be the final test of my doings there, and my endeavour as a sensible woman was to live as irreproachable as possible. With this aim from the first, I was willing to make myself agreeable to every one, so far as it was consistent with my ideas of right and wrong. So when Mrs. Sutton seemed anxious to get me to talk, I showed myself quite willing to do so ; or to refrain, when I saw the least want of interest.

Ann, the cook, was a Catholic. She went when I did, and consequently had not been there long. One day, a sister of Mrs. Sutton's, who was on a visit, came to me and asked if I did not think we should talk to Ann, or do something to get her to change her religion. I was startled by the question, but after a moment's thought, replied, "Do you think we can make Ann a better girl by doing so?" This was not spoken without knowledge. I had been struck from the first with Ann's diligent use of the means of her church for worship. On Sunday mornings in winter, she would rise before any one else in the house, and start off fasting before it was light, all weathers, to walk three miles to her chapel, to hear early mass. She would stay to the morning service, coming back about two o'clock, without breaking her fast. She would then at once relieve the other girl, and take the work of both, in consideration of having herself been out in the morning.

From the nursery, as the long days advanced, I

have often seen her kneeling by her bed in prayerful
attitude. I could see this unknown to her; and
many a time her zeal put to shame my own more
lax and uncertain devotions. Heaven help me!
Her ignorance outstripped my better knowledge, in
the practical worship of God, as it may be that of
many another has done whom I have foolishly
condemned! Besides this, Ann was a thoroughly
good servant; a clever cook, upright and careful,
respecting all her mistress's wishes.

So the lady, knowing this much, left me without
saying another word. And I stood wondering how
it was that so wise an answer to her had so suddenly
been given me. I ought to say, perhaps, that this
Catholic servant lived in this Quaker family for ten
years, treated by them with much confidence and
respect; the humble friend of themselves and the
children, and yet she never changed her religion.
Indeed, as I have grown older, I have come to see
and feel that creeds are less than life. The latter
may be true, when the former is far from it. The
force of creeds, however, is very great.

I remember some years after this, having been
introduced to an Italian lady in Carlisle—a public

singer, a Madame Cora de Stella—as a person interested in German poetry and literature. I found her an exceedingly well read person, and especially interested in what I said of some of the great thinkers of Germany—Jacobi Novalis, Schiller, and others. She also indulged in some remarks on their religious views, in which she expressed herself as deeply interested, but added, clasping her hands together, "Oh, Miss Smith! when I take a silent walk in the fields or by the river side, and grow sad and prayerful, it is always my mother's prayer which rises in my soul—that and no other." Did I reprove this lady, or try to change her faith? I did no such thing. That she really prayed at all, was enough for me.

CHAPTER XI.

I was henceforth very happy at Scotby. I continued as usual all my duties in the nursery, neither asking nor taking any liberties of any kind; too proud for that; only taking care to do all that was required of me. Sitting closely at sewing, making all manner of things for the children, from frocks and tippets for common wear, to almost everything else that was needed, till nine o'clock in the evening.

I had myself adopted this hour for giving over work, and strictly adhered to it all the time I was at Scotby; though Mrs. Sutton would occasionally come in bringing a daily newspaper for me to read, bidding me put my work aside.

One Sunday when it was my turn to go to chapel, it was such a flood of rain that I was prevented. Mrs. Sutton brought me a lot of books from their library to choose from. Only one could I find to interest me, Howitt's "History of Civilization," a book it is worth any one's while to read and ponder over.

At this time I first became acquainted with the writings of Thomas Carlyle. Emerson and he thenceforth became my two great masters of thought for the rest of my life. Carlyle's gospel of Work and exposure of Shams, and his universal onslaught on the nothings and appearances of society, gave strength and life to my vague but true enthusiasm. They proved a new Bible of blessedness to my eager soul, as they did to thousands beside, who had become weary of much of the vapid literature of the time. I read all his works I could get hold of, and my poems will testify how truly I appreciated them.

One day Mr. Sutton asked me if I knew what the critics said about Carlyle; perhaps wishing to suggest that I should read him with caution, as the Friends at that time considered his teachings as somewhat sceptical. I replied, I knew quite well, but did not heed them; believing they were prejudiced against him, some through want of comprehension, and others through pure ignorance.

About this time, I possessed myself of a small edition of Emerson's Essays. I carried it in my pocket for many years, so that whenever I had a little spare time, I took up this source of instruction and inspiration. By reading them over and over, in this way, which I did with increasing delight, I came to know him almost entirely by heart, and could quote him largely without any trouble.

I also carried about pocket editions of the poets in the same way and for the same purpose. Especially I remember having done so with Tom Moore, hoping to catch something of his exquisite melody, for I knew well enough my verses wanted music, and that however full of thought they might be, it was the music that constituted the song qualities.

In Longfellow I found much my heart craved, as I believe thousands of others did, for it is ever the religious sentiment that best satisfies the human heart, and commands the deepest and truest devotion and love. I read his stirring stanzas in newspapers and periodicals, and such was their effect at first, that I could not sleep for repeating them and thinking of them. The "Psalm of Life," "Sand of the Desert," and the "Ladder of St. Augustine," were the first I happened to see, and never shall I forget the vivid enthusiastic life they awakened in me. Night and day they were in my thoughts, though not in my speech, as I had no literary friend at Scotby, save and except Mrs. Sutton herself. With her I had earnest and interesting talk at intervals, I believe as much to her delight as my own, for intellect knows no rank.

I had two or three admirers at this period, but I only heard of them through my friends the Osborns. Here is a little story somewhat amusing. I was up at my friends' for my "term,"* as it is called, at which time I generally did my shopping. Mrs. Osborn and I were in the sitting room in the evening of a late autumn night, when their landlord, Mr. So-and-So, came in, a well-to-do tradesman, and widower. Inviting him to wait Mr. Osborn's return, I was introduced to him as a young friend of the family. He stayed a full hour or more, during which time Mrs. Osborn kept him engaged in conversation, for she was a grand talker. When he rose to depart, I—as was proper—though I had

---

* In the north of England, Whitsuntide and Martinmas are the "term" times for domestic servants, that is, the holidays which intervene between one half-year and the other.—*Ed.*

neither looked up from my work nor spoken—again stood up to say "Good-night."

Judge then of my surprise, on my next visit, when Mrs. Osborn told me that Mr. So-and-So had fallen in love with me. He had asked her to have him to tea with me, so that he might have an opportunity of making me an offer. I at once exclaimed: "No, it's no use. I cannot do that." I could see all my intellectual castles falling with a crash, to rise no more. And, moreover, I had formed the opinion, that to marry for earthly advantage, without one's affections being intertwined, was a foul blot which nothing could justify. So though she remonstrated with me, calling me foolish, and saying he was a good man (which was true enough), I still said: "No, it's impossible! He's not intellectual. What is marriage *without* happiness! The bare idea of it is dreadful to contemplate."

I never saw this gentleman again till many years after, when I met him casually at a tea-party. He recognised me with a merry twinkle in his eye, thinking evidently of that ancient tea at which we had met, before his head had grown grizzled and bare. He was very polite, and thanked me for the kindness which he said I had shown his daughter, whom I had accidentally met on a day's excursion to Derwentwater. I always respected him, but never regretted my action. Thus are romance and hard facts interwoven with our lives.

The ordinary routine of this Quaker family very much resembled that of my own home. The same reverent quiet spirit pervaded all the house. There was no scolding; no storms of any kind between husband and wife. His wishes were studied and observed from morning to night. " William likes it so," was continually on his wife's lips in arranging for the day, and in giving orders to the servants. She was, in fact, a model wife, exerting herself continually to do whatever he required.

Starting on a journey, either by night or day, she saw to all his luggage; everything being put where it could easily be found. And when going by the midnight train, she alone sat up and saw him start off.

The children were rather spoken to than scolded, and prompt obedience was expected at all times. In their behaviour to the servants, and any one under them, very rigid rules were enforced. Nothing was to be taken or done for them by a servant, without the ready "Thank thee," or "Obliged to thee," as soon as they were able to articulate the words.

Mrs. Sutton was at all times very particular about the truth, especially in those who had anything to do with the little ones. Once when they had a younger under-nurse, she came to me and asked, "Dost thou think Lizzie always speaks the truth?" Indeed it did a girl good to be there awhile. One girl called to see the children, some months after leaving, and when I enquired how she was doing, said, with tears in her eyes, "Ah! I should have stayed here. You are all so quiet, and so happy, and contented."

The Quakers had no tricks or sleight of hand for getting money. They earned what they got, by dint of rigid punctuality, plunging deep into business, and they themselves seeing and knowing how every thing came and went. They were very hard to cheat, or to get the upper hand of in anything. A half-day's fishing in Wetheral woods, with the Rev. J. Halifax, the vicar, who lived close by, was the only relaxation which Mr. Sutton took. And in their expenditure, there was no show. They held that money must be earned before it was spent. Not the modern plan of spending first, and paying —or not—afterward.

Fashion followed afar off, and kept a very demure face there. And then the old Quaker ladies at Scotby, with their peach-white satin poke bonnets and dresses, and beautiful spun silk drab shawls, devoid of fringe ; with their "thee's" and "thou's," and their sweetly lipped "farewells," and their calmly bright effulgent faces, like pictures, always the same, have mostly passed away now. Yet like all pure and beautiful things, they have left precious memories behind them.

I had been at Scotby nearly a year, when going to chapel every fortnight, I was regularly supplied with literary and religious gossip, and learnt that some of my friends had been sending verses to Whitridge's *Miscellany*. Oddly enough my own mind had often run in that direction, when left to myself in the nursery in a morning. Busy with my hands, I found, as I often before had done, that by concentrating the mind on some single subject, I could throw my thoughts into verse as an exercise.

And by doing this, I could relieve myself of the feeling that, do what I could, I was living a sad, monotonous, profitless life, so far as anything I specially desired or wished for was concerned.

But in engaging my mind, while my hands were fully occupied, I began regularly to pursue my own thoughts, with great zeal and delight, during that time, as my capacity to do so seemed to grow amain with every new opportunity. I composed in this way many trifles, as mere mental exercises. The action improved and quickened my mind. With Dr. Arnold, I would recommend everyone to keep a verse book, though, like him, they never think of printing their verses.

I wrote on for many months, never naming it, with the exception of taking a copy of such as related to any event in my friends' family. These pieces were read and admired. I was told by the Rev. W. J. Tweddle, who had become a Wesleyan preacher, that he often quoted my verses in the Manchester and Liverpool pulpits. Thus many of my earlier verses became known and read, being lent and copied; and I went on, as the poet always does, to produce others. One, "A Starless Night," my friends sent to the *Miscellany*, which was to come next after a piece of James Milligan's. This arrangement filled the mind of the poor stammering weaver with gratitude and delight.

However, contrary to my wish, an incident occurred over this little poem, which annoyed me. The *Miscellany* was taken at Scotby I found, and as these were my first printed verses, I did not quite know when they would appear. Consequently one evening, Mrs. Sutton came running to me to ask, much to my surprise, if the verses signed "M..S." were mine. I at once said "Yes," though not quite pleased to have my secret known. In apology, she said she knew they were, as they were so like the way I talked; but for my comfort, she did not seem at all displeased. I did not wish to talk about them, only thinking them very moderate, so on that subject we spoke no more.

In the first verses of mine, sent to the *Carlisle Journal* by my friends, the initials were misprinted; the "M.S." being "M.L.," which hid my secret. This piece was entitled "The Good Time Coming" Charles Mackay's song, under the same title, was being sung everywhere just then, by all sorts of people. To my practical mind there did not appear to be much wisdom in it. So I tried to write one on the same subject.

It's a good time now for all to strive,
    And effort maketh stronger:
Oh, let us up—man maketh the times—
    Let us up and wait no longer.

This may perhaps show that my verse, if deficient in music and beauty, had from the first back-bone in it. Poetry, in fact, grew into a passion with me. I soon found I must be on my guard against it. I could not afford to neglect the duties of my situation, and the moral responsibilities connected therewith. "Better write no poetry at all, than lower myself to do wrong," I said to myself. So I wanted no mistress' eye upon me. My own was enough; and many a little lecture I read myself on being faithful in all things.

But, alas! a very small circumstance showed what dangerous ways I was treading. One day, when I was busy in the nursery, Mrs. Sutton called to me for a shawl once or twice, but I did not hear her. At last, Mary Ann, the servant, came running to fetch it. Had I not heard Mrs. Sutton calling to me over and over for it? she asked. And did I not hear her when she spoke to me in the morning before? My shame-faced reply was "No," and seizing the shawl in her hands, I at once leaped down to Mrs. Sutton with it. I told her I was very sorry indeed, but I really had not heard her. I certainly would try and be more careful in future.

She looked coldly incredulous; but if she was vexed with me, I was a thousand times more vexed with myself. My pride had had an awful fall before them all, and I wished to make no excuse. The greatest trouble to me was that my word should be doubted, as it had been, both by Mrs. Sutton and Mary Ann. But I made no protestation. It was the first time I had been lost in thought to such an extent. I must take care to be on my guard. I must poetise only in the evening, when the children were in bed.

Never again while I was there did I allow any one to speak to me without hearing them. In after years, however, I have frequently been told of meeting friends, even on the street, whom I have not recognised, and of having been spoken to when I have not heard; but my friends knew and understood me then, and wisely let me go my own way.

One day, Mrs. Sutton came into the back parlour, when I was with the children at lessons, and one of them spoke to me as "Smith" in her presence. She turned to me, and said, "Oh dear, I do not like to hear them call thee that hard name. I wish we could call thee something else." I was silent for a moment. I had been called "Miss Smith" ever since I had left home, and often before. I knew the Friends objected to titles, so I said, call me "Governess" if you like. She went away without further remark, but the next day I found the servants had orders to call me "Governess;" the children and their parents being the first to do so.

But I had no vanity about these things. My hopes and aspirations lay in another direction, towards which I was apparently making no progress. My solace and joy being in the fact that I was still able to devote my time of leisure, though little, to reading and reflection, with seasons also of verse making. My great aim was to use simple, natural language, avoiding metaphors as Wordsworth did, and never to write without a feeling of help and inspiration. My path had never been strewn with roses, and whatever I attempted to do, I felt must be done without encouragement.

It was about the second year of my being at
Scotby that I sent some poems to the *People's
Journal*. I did this at first as a test of what they
were worth, as I had no one whose judgment I
could rely on. "Look Up" was the title of the
first one thus published—

Heaven's holy missionaries, the stars, come every night,
And talk of God and destiny in the language of light;
And walk we with downcast eyes? Are their wondrous
    words unread?
Their voices all unheard? O Man, lift, lift thy bowed head.

I wrote these poems and many others under the
nom de plume of "Mary Osborn," solely for the
purpose of remaining unknown in the family where
I was. I feared they might think I neglected some
duty to attend to them, though really this was not
the case. They were mostly composed while engaged in some duty that left my mind free, or
oftener while on the road between Carlisle and
Scotby, going or returning from chapel.

To return to my life at Scotby. It was in every
way a great mental growth and peaceful pleasure.
My duty was to my liking, and I was trusted
implicitly, the keys being left with me and the

care of all in Mrs. Sutton's absence. The second summer I was there, we went to Flimby, on the west Cumberland coast, for six weeks. This was a great joy to me, as I had never seen the open sea before. The sea and the mountains together made a deep impression on my mind; the one enhancing and giving life to the other. The waves were within hearing day and night. And it was an exquisite pleasure to walk along the lovely coast as far as Maryport, which I often did about sunset to the Baptist chapel, the sea and sky then putting on all their solemn grandeur and glory.

I have seen bits of the sea at seaside towns since, but have been generally disgusted at its draggled and defiled appearance. Indeed, I saw nothing that came up to the coast scenery about Flimby. The night before we left was full moon, and very clear. Mrs. Sutton thought it would interest me to go and see the sea at midnight, poet like, under the silvery light of the moon. I went, and saw one of the fairest sights I ever beheld or hope to behold in this world. Our free mode of life at Flimby put new strength into us all, and we returned home very happy and contented.

I had unbounded peace and comfort at Scotby, and therefore thought I could never be better off. I was not one of those sanguine souls who believe in future, instead of living in the present. I had no complaints, fearing rather that I might be complained of, although the marked kindness I was shown continually convinced me to the contrary.

My days had little variation; all were alike calm and happy, the common events merely of household life. Visitors at intervals came and went, and small parties of Friends made a show of company in the best rooms of the house, and now and then a flutter among the servants. Some passing celebrities came to dinner, who might be holding a meeting or lecturing in Carlisle. The Friends were in advance of most people in politics and the popular topics of the day. So we had James Silk Buckingham, whom I went to hear lecture; and Henry Vincent, whose style of eloquence was of the most robust and manly order.

Coming home from a political gathering one night, Mr. Sutton said to me, that they wanted a first rate speaker for a coming meeting. Did I know of one? I replied, at once, "Send for

Henry Vincent.   He will please you all."   He had
fascinated me (as the first political speaker I had
heard), when he contested the borough of Banbury.
Happening to be with a cousin of mine—in spite
of her remonstrances—I would stop and hear him
answer George Harris, on the steps of the "Flying
Horse" yard, although I dare not tell my father.
Vincent was a Chartist, which at that time was a
name of terror to many people.   At Carlisle he
seemed to captivate everybody, and to sway the
vast audience at his will.

We had other notables, and, by times, much
interesting talk on politics.   I was at Scotby
through the year 1848, and we shared all the
excitement of the great world in that small northern
village, rejoicing with the best when unkingly kings
were uncrowned.

George Dawson of Birmingham came to lecture
on George Fox at Carlisle.   We went to hear him.
He shocked the old friends with his free speech
and outspoken truthfulness, especially when he told
them that "George Fox would spew the modern
Quakers out of his mouth!"   When I got home,
Mrs. Sutton asked what I thought of that.   I said

what I believed, which was, that I thought it true, and still think so, too.

George Fox and the early Friends were among the truest, noblest, and most courageous saints of all the ages; and in their aim at sincerity of speech, action, and worship, they inaugurated one of the greatest and most practical reforms since the Christian era.

In truth, we lived a sort of Arcadian life at Scotby. Our conversation, and small excitements, though limited, being of the best order. We kept our sympathies, as well as our intelligence, up to the stroke of the great world, and shared the cares of its life struggles.

I asked for few liberties. My own friends were in Oxfordshire, too far for me to have visited them if I had wished, and here I had none to take counsel from; but so far as that was concerned, I was satisfied. I had got to love the children very much, especially the little twin I had had from her birth, who had become to me as dear as my own child.

CHAPTER XII.

BUT the happiest periods come to an end, as did
this one at Scotby. My old friends at Carlisle,
who for many years were a fate to me, had got into
trouble. Mr. Osborn preached doctrines which
the Baptist Society deemed unsound, and notice
came that the grant would be withdrawn. It was
withdrawn accordingly, and the church was too
poor to support him without it. What were they
to do? "Begin a school," said their friends. But
Mr. Osborn had never done anything of the kind,
and it was to be a mixed school, as nearly all the
schools are in the north.

The next Sunday I went to Carlisle, therefore, I
was asked if I would leave Scotby, and help them
in the proposed school, as in that way they felt
sure of success. It was a great surprise for me,
and I felt from past experience, that it would be
against all my best interests, and would be a sore
trial to me. But then, here was a family of young

children actually starving, not enough to eat, as I knew, and the mother near her confinement. What was I to do? I took a week to think of it, and much as my mind was against it, the wan faces of those children who had to be limited every day and denied food, haunted me continually. I dare not refuse to come to their aid.

I was promised the same wage which I had at Scotby, if the school succeeded. The school did well, but I never received any salary. The result was that I spent the little I had saved, wore out all my clothes, and offended even my poor father, who wanted me to stay where I was well off. But I was religious, and had on principle refused to be the wife of a well-to-do man, for whom I had no affection; and I now thought it my duty to go in the face of my friends and my own interests to try to save this starving family, to whose poor children I was much attached.

Never shall I forget what I felt when I told Mrs. Sutton I would be obliged to leave, nor shall I forget the agitation it caused her. They saw it was done out of a sense of duty. The first words Mrs. Sutton said were—they had not given me money enough, and Mr. Sutton would give me anything I wished. I at once told her everything—told her that money was not in my thoughts at all—far otherwise. So they let me go, seeing my mind was definitely made up.

Our school was in a house at the bottom of Castle-street, now occupied by Mr. Robert Dalton, auctioneer. There I lived and laboured for more than a year.

Mr. Osborn had the reputation of being very clever, and really was so in many things. He had the best of all gifts, that of inspiring young men with faith in themselves and with what they could do. He was also very kind with the younger ones, and stood less upon his dignity than most masters, which made him popular alike with the children and their parents. He was well recommended, as he had given lessons for some time to gentlemen in grammar, logic, elocution, etc. He had also published a sixpenny chart of grammar, very useful to local preachers and others; and a sixpenny handbook of logic, for the working men of his former classes, to whom these manuals had been very useful. These stood him in good stead in beginning his school.

In a short time, the school room was filled with children of the well-to-do classes of the city, so that there was no longer any fear of success. But I was the practical teacher in all the classes, for even the biggest boys soon found that I could answer their questions and understood their work as well as their master. In fact, I was at times left with the whole school of sixty or seventy boys and girls, for a day together, while Mr. Osborn was out on other business. I had both a laborious and responsible situation.

This was rendered especially so, when I had pupils of an evening, which I occasionally had. I was sometimes engaged three evenings in a week. I did the teaching, though he made the bills out and took the money; and this mode of procedure also held good of the evening pupils I had. I was indeed worked so hard and kept so close while there, that all through summer I was never able to get out for a walk in the evening, nor indeed at any other time, save Sunday afternoon. At times, my head was excruciating, and all sorts of remedies had to be tried for it. But besides hard work, I had also very scant and coarse fare, which, it is true, I very often volunteered to take, knowing they were very hard up and deep in debt. I believe I would have gone entirely without food of any kind, could I have done it, so anxious was I to get them set forward on a better footing.

But bad as these things were, they were not those that tried me the most, or made me feel the keenest. There was an atmosphere of jealousy, I felt, continually around and about me, that led to criticising and underrating very much, if not all, I did. This was carried so far, at times, as to lead to my being found fault with, and rebuked before the whole school, which—after being so much respected at Scotby—tried me very much.

In the old days, when I was young and strong, I was very much of a Spartan. At Scotby, I refused all luxuries that were offered me, and took only the plainest food. I had done without luxuries in Westmorland, and thought it both wise and well to school myself by plain living, remembering that one "eats to live" only, and that it is nobler to make one's wants few than many.

So for me to do without animal food for weeks together, as I then did, was less trying than it would have been to many, especially as I often volunteered to do so for the sake of others. Still as they knew I was doing this entirely for their good, and keeping it all a secret to myself, I certainly did expect some little respect. But a woman without friends in the world, as I was, must harden herself to dare and endure much.

I was not, however, joyless among my hard work and sorrow. I carried a pocket edition of Emerson always about with me in those days, nor could I possibly have had a better book, as he teaches the truths of social heroism as none other. One morning, I remember, I had this book open in my hand, at "Heroism," as I sat at breakfast. Mr. Osborn coming down, passed behind me, and paused to look over my shoulder. He had done so on other mornings. Finding me still at the same subject, it seems, for he exclaimed, "What! Heroism again, Mary?"

Yes, certainly, I needed to be schooled in heroism, more than anything else. For beside long hours of teaching, I had the school-room to sweep and dust, every morning before breakfast; and on Saturdays, to assist in all the work of the house. Sometimes, in fact, I was rather glad, on a Saturday, to have a room to scrub, as then I was left to myself, and could compose while I cleaned, if so inclined. In this way, nearly the whole of the poem "Simple Flowers" was cast into shape one Saturday. Very happy was I on these occasions, as the inspiration of my mind lightened the labour of my hands; and that little poem, which appeared in one of Cassell's Magazines, I always considered one of my best.

It arose from the fact of my having seen some pretty flowers growing in the window at my old French teacher's in a lane in Scotch-street, the night before. Many of my poems, all through life, were composed in the same way, or in taking a lonely walk in the country.

But to me there was another and brighter side of my life, without which, perhaps, I hardly could have endured so much. This French lesson, two evenings a week, proved a very interesting and novel pleasure to me. The old lady, a Miss Patrickson, had many amusing traits in her some-what Frenchified demeanour. She attended the Bible Society's meetings held at Rickerby house, in George Head Head's time, and once called upon me in her gala get up, as she went there, like herself in nothing but her French ways.

She was about sixty years old, and had been in Paris a dozen years. Had seen much of its literary society, especially of Monsieur de Balzac, with whom she had been on intimate terms. She had translated several of his novels, so she told me, and which seemed quite possible, from her manners and conversation. She had an endless store of anecdote and story about the novelist and his compeers, which she was constantly telling me, more than half of which was spoken in French.

This I knew to be very helpful to me, and so I wisely let her run on. You seemed to be in a Parisian boudoir. In fact, her literary assumptions, and the endless shrug of her shoulders, were very piquant; and she contrived to show some bit of brightness, in the shape of cap and shawl, however deficient otherwise. Her door (which I usually found barred), and certain potent smells (which I invariably found floating in the air), led me to think that she cheered her solitude with other than literary stimulants. But I never knew that this was literally the case. The heart knoweth its own bitterness, and there is no doubt she needed comfort in her loneliness.

I always treated her with deference, and she in return prepared and illustrated my lessons with much care. Her pronunciation was very good. Every time I went, I got her to give me a French dictation lesson. This I found was capital for the pronunciation, as it obliged me to give very close attention to her manner of speaking, and led her to pronounce it as slowly and deliberately as possible; often, to help me, doing so twice over. In this way, better than any other, I became familiarised with the words of my lesson.

I worked resolutely in school and out, always employed, whoever else was gadding about, or whatever was going on in the city. Parents as well as children soon got to know that I was the better and more painstaking teacher of the two, where pains and patience were really needed. Hence I became very popular among the pupils, especially with the boys, whose work, they soon found, I knew all about.

But in spite of all the hard work, we often had

very pleasant evenings. Mr. Osborn was certainly an intellectual man. He had the gift of attracting men of the same character, of stimulating their abilities, and developing their aspirations, though himself a very partially educated man. Could he have remained a preacher, it would have been more favourable to his upward progress, though he had in him an element of change, which deteriorated from that stability and strength required to build up a truly wise and good man.

Many young men of good parts, drawn by Mr. Osborn's abilities, gathered up in the evenings for talk and discussion. Among these were Dr. Robert Elliot, Mr. J. A. Cockburn, Mr. W. J. Tweddle, Mr. D. Blackburn, and many more. Dr. Elliot was one of the most intelligent, as well as one of the latest sitters—often continuing his discourse over night till late in the morning. He had infinite resources of conversation. He was a great observer and an acute reasoner, and was well skilled in scientific research.

Night after night there would be discussions on some set subject, such as theology, science, logic, or politics. Being frequently invited to take part in these discussions, I sometimes did so. I was as well up in logic as most of them, but preferred to find the basis of truth in something more godlike than logic. Hence I refused to yield full credence to its decisions. Logic alone does not answer the question—what is Truth? The inspired soul of man alone can do that, hence I had no regard for hard and dry logical conclusions. I always held fast to my primary conclusions, that a man must himself be divinely true, before his conclusions can be so.

Nor did we hold merely intellectual discussions. All the popular topics of the day came under our notice. New books were talked of and criticised, and special historic events, such as Lord John Russell's "No Popery" letter, which caused a tremendous amount of talk among all sorts and conditions of people.

Mr. Osborn sided with the Catholics, as most of us did; but I thought he should have been more independent than to have allowed himself to be seated in Mr. Phillip Howard's carriage to speak for them. I told him so, as I remember, when he came home late at night, after attending an excited meeting which had been held on the Sands. The "larger heart" proved the truer one, as in history it has ever done. Would that we could learn that fact! Pity that Lord John, with his own heretical proclivities, should have sounded so narrow and false a note.

And what a sensation some books created! The Oxford tracts had been published and read before this; but John Henry Newman was now before the public, with his "Sorrows of the Soul" and "Phases of Faith," both of which came to Mr. Osborn's house.

But the book that most excited the wonder and curiosity of the reading world of that time, and, as religious people then said, filled them with scepticism, was one of a quite different type. This was the "Vestiges of Creation." I doubt not that it loosened some of the strongholds of the literal and plenary inspiration views of the Bible; and, it might be, weakened imperceptibly some of that terrible gravity of thought and feeling which Calvinists, and indeed most truly religious people, regarded at that time the truths of religion.

Calvinism was a sober truth with millions of

people up till then. There were many of all
denominations who lived daily in the fear of hell;
and scepticism of the archfiend's personal power
was then considered equal in its wickedness to the
doubt of Deity and a future state. Judge then the
alarm and head-shaking this book was received
with in the religious world. Many of them read it
clandestinely, and then silently waited for the
comments and criticisms of the press and pulpit.

The book came as a loan to 84 Castle-street.
Its incredible statements, as I got to know something of them from others, made me intensely
anxious to read it for myself. To this end, I got
hold of the book one night. It was in the long
days of summer. Not being able to read it otherwise, I sat up till after daybreak, finishing its
interesting pages by the first light of the morning,
at my bedroom window.

On myself and my mode of thought, this book,
and its successors in the same field, effected little
change. Its arguments were to me much harder to
believe than the dear old truths of the Bible, and
the divine doctrines of the New Testament. These
latter revive and quicken and inspire the spirit of

man, thus proving their truth, as the organ of vision proves the light of day. Like Thomas Carlyle, my own early life owed its best and brightest influences to the devout Calvinism under which it was reared. Religion, I think, has little to fear from scientific inquiry, or its endlessly changing theories of nature and man.

I wrote but two or three poems during the year I was at Castle-street, as I worked tremendously all day and every day, and often far into the night. It was while seated at my small table, poring over my books at midnight, that I was roused into full consciousness of their beauty, by the cathedral chimes striking full and clear upon me at that hour. This event led to my composing a short piece on the subject, then and there. It was sent to the *Carlisle Journal*, and as it appeared without a name, simply "84 Castle-street," it was universally attributed to Mr. Osborn.

But I found at the school and in the house, whatever I did I failed to please. My patience, hard work, and endurance of unjust criticism were all in vain. I was needlessly made to feel affronts for which there was no excuse, and slighted day after day without any possible reason. Any new or interesting book, I found, was put into a drawer and locked up, contrary to custom, and much to my mortification: I was piqued continually with petty annoyances.

Notwithstanding these things, I had an unusually strong and sincere attachment to the Osborns, and should hardly have considered any sacrifice too great to make on their behalf. This attachment to the family had now been strengthened by the years I had been with or near them.

I found all the parents of the scholars very kind to me. One lady, a Mrs. William Wood, who had children at school, made me a present of a new dress. I have no doubt, by my dilapidated appearance, she had guessed the secret of my working for nothing. But I shrank from eliciting such acts as these. My friends were offended by these favours to me. They seemed to imply a reflection on them, and did not increase my comfort at home.

Amid all things time flies. At the midsummer holidays, I had been a year with them. The school had become a thoroughly good one; and I was now told, not very gratefully, that they could do without me, and that I could go home if I wished. It was the arrangement that I was to have fifteen pounds for the year, but as yet I had been paid nothing. Instead of this I was reminded of the privileges I had enjoyed. I had gone out for my French for an hour, two evenings a week, and had the advantage of reading various works, especially two volumes of Fichte. It was unkindly said I had soiled these volumes, and in consequence I agreed to take them as part of my salary. But nothing more was ever offered me, and I had not the courage to demand it as I ought.

CHAPTER XIII.

In the meantime, my father had written for me to go home, if I were disengaged, as I had now been away nearly ten years, seeing no one belonging to me all that time. It was a long and expensive journey, and one I could by no means afford to undertake. My money had diminished, till I had barely enough to pay my fare back into Oxfordshire, even by taking the cheapest route from Whitehaven to Liverpool. I was disappointed, weary, and sad, and needed rest. I longed to see my dear father, who I knew still believed in me and loved me He had not approved of my leaving Scotby, seeing clearly that in my ready generosity, I was running against my own interest, which I could hardly afford to do.

So with a very low purse and a sad heart— leaving the furniture of my bedroom behind me, nor asking for my salary due, nor the balance borrowed from me in Westmorland—I left Carlisle, and embarked from Whitehaven at ten o'clock at night for Liverpool, which latter place we reached about half-past five next morning.

It was the year of the first great Exhibition in London of 1851, and there were many passengers on board. It was the first time I had been on the sea, and consequently I was very sick, as was another young lady who, with her brother, was travelling to the great exhibition. We found it a very trying voyage, and I mentally vowed, if spared to reach land, I would never take another voyage on the sea.

I took the train from Birkenhead to Birmingham in the morning, where I had a brother living, and was glad to remain with him a few days before going further. The sea sickness had turned me very yellow. The hard work and hard fare, and the almost total want of fresh air and animal food, of which in early days I had enjoyed an unstinted supply, had had their due effect on my form and features, which were by no means flattering. I looked, by the aid of this final incident, rather like a person recovering from a fever, and quite unlike the stout, fresh coloured, **blooming country girl I was when I left home.**

The result was, that when I reached my native village, hardly anyone out of my own family knew me. One young woman, who had lived at the school to which I went, and had known me intimately, curtsied to me profoundly as I walked down the village street, and on my turning and exclaiming "Mary," could hardly believe her own eyes. "Why," I said, "who did you think I was?" To which she replied, "The vicar's wife." So it seems I had acquired in slender gentility what I had lost in country buxomness.

A day or two after, when I called to see an old lady, a neighbour and friend of our family, she exclaimed on seeing me, "Why, Mary, wherever have you been? Where is that place? Why, I shouldn't have known you. You were a nice girl before you went away—and now you are quite spoil't." Alas! it was quite true, so far as my looks were concerned. My good looks, if such I ever had, had vanished 'neath hard work and study, spare diet, and the pressure of hard town life. But thank God—as I do to this day—I had come back untarnished by crime of any kind.

After nearly ten years' absence, I began in a few

weeks to feel very much out of my element at home, as I had no occupation. I became anxious, even very eager for something to do, for I had but a shilling or two left. So I looked over all manner of advertisements, seeking an assistant teacher's or preparatory governess's situation; for alas! I had no accomplishments, so called. No music, nor singing, nor dancing; no German, Italian, and very little French; nor any fine manners.

I was simply an uncorrupted girl, with a plain education, who knew thoroughly grammar, geography, practical arithmetic, and the general run of things then taught in respectable middle class schools. Besides, I was brimful of knowledge, which had been gathered from my vast and multifarious reading in history, science and literature. But I was dismayed. Every advertisement I read, even for farmers' families in the country, required music and French, and the various accompaniments of what was called "genteel education."

But it gratified the vanity of ignorant parents, who were able to boast of their daughters having learned French. Their music did not fare much better, as it was rare to find a piano, or even har-

monium, in country farm houses at that period.
The farming class did not understand the need of
practice, so that in all but exceptional cases the
young "miss" who had got a bit of music at the
boarding school, soon lost it for the want of an
instrument to practice on.   But what then?   The
old mother, who dressed in black silk, with flowing
lace veil, could boast that "Mary Ann" had learnt
French and music at the boarding school.   Its real
end—a sad one—being to make her think she
should keep her hands white, her ringlets always
in curl, and wear her good dresses every day, as
she did when she went to school.

To return to my story.   With this state of things,
I did not find it easy to get a situation, as they all
wanted more than I could honestly promise.   It is
true, I was continually writing after some situation,
and continually being disappointed.   My father
perceiving this, said: "You have a good home.
Why not remain where you are?"   He, at least,
was glad of my company.

In those bright summer evenings, after I had sat
in my room all day studying French grammar and
French history, I found it very sweet to sally forth

up the dear old country roads, to meet him coming home with the pony and trap from his rounds of registration, paying the poor of the parish, etc. Of course I got a ride home with him, under the large and beautiful trees, which in Oxfordshire adorn everywhere the broad grassy roads, whose tall luxuriant hedgerows were then fragrant with their garlands of summer flowers.

Our talk was often somewhat sad, for I was daily disappointed of some situation or other. He had a patient ear for all my little confidences, and was always ready with some hopeful Scripture word of encouragement and cheer. "Ah! my wench," he often said, "we are like Jacob of old. We often say, 'All these things are against us,' but could we see further and clearer we should see that they are all for our good."

We are poor judges of the eternal providence, indeed, as since then I have often found out For instance, I did not perceive then what renewed health and strength I was getting from my long summer rest at Cropredy, nor how I was enlarging my mental resources by my unrestricted study of French while there.

After I had been at home some two months, my studies were agreeably interrupted by my younger brother, George, then unmarried, who had been successful in business, and who was, in fact, the very reverse of myself in most things, proposing to take me, with a party of other friends, to see the Great Exhibition of 1851. At the same time, he generously said I need not think anything about the expense, as he would pay everything. My father and mother both urged me to accept the proposal, knowing that he had the means to do it.

So some time about the latter end of August of that year, we started off on a week's excursion to London, to see this latest wonder of the world. We travelled—as everybody did—by an excursion train, the first I had any experience of, and all our party were very weary of it. So long was it on the road, so wretchedly full of coarse ill-mannered people, so small attention was given by officials, and so long and frequent the delays we had to endure. We started before twelve o'clock at noon from Banbury, a journey I suppose of about seventy miles, and did not get to London till past eleven at night.

I felt this all the more, as I had left home in pain

from indigestion. However, George, who was much disgusted, declared he would not travel back by that mode whatever he paid. On this account, we decided to return by the other line, and have a little time at Oxford, to see the ancient city and its famous colleges, which we did.

We had comfortable lodgings at an hotel in Charterhouse-square, the proprietor of which was a near relative to one or two of our party. Country folks as we were, we naturally made the exhibition our first object, setting off for Hyde Park directly after breakfast, about nine o'clock, so as to be there when the doors opened. We went in with the common people on the shilling day; though in our round of the immense palace we met many of our rich neighbours, country folks as a rule being careful of their money, and anxious to get things as cheaply as they can.

We exhausted our morning in wandering everywhere over this arena of art, in our anxiety to see *all,* and were glad to sit down near the large fountain, and get an early lunch. We found it a good opportunity for taking mental notes of the moving myriads passing continually before us of all nations, peoples, kindred, and tongues, for such in reality they were. Thoroughly tired, we took our meal leisurely for rest, drawing our liquor from the sparkling fountain near us, in glasses we had brought with us.

That over, and reinvigorated by it, we struck out in another direction, and came upon a world of wonders of mechanical skill. One of these was a bedstead so contrived that it could be set like an alarum to any hour desired, and at that time would begin, by springs, to fold itself up, and throw the sleeper out of bed. This feat was being constantly performed by the originator, to merry crowds of passing visitors, among whom our party were detained for a few minutes.

My brother gave me a nudge to look in a certain direction where, quite near us, stood an old blind woman, as much interested and as merry as the rest, as she heard the unfortunate occupant of the bed thrown out on the floor. The simple party she was with, probably sons and daughters from some remote country district, telling and explaining all to her. Indeed, we almost met with as much to interest us in the motley multitude of people we passed, as in the great world's show itself. Sometimes their ignorance, and sometimes their mistakes, being so amusing and odd. But everybody was pleased and in good humour. It was better than all the "plays." It was what Englishmen like, especially the middle classes. It was a great reality, a thing to be seen and talked about for a life-time; a kind of Queen of Sheba's shop, with all the stores of the great world in it.

Our temperate way of arranging our sightseeing did not cost us very much, though we saw nearly all the wonders of London. We were at St. Paul's Cathedral on Sunday afternoon, and at Madame Tussaud's on Monday, which was well worth seeing, though I dare not venture into the chamber of horrors, nor see any of its criminals. My imagination was such that I could never have forgotten them, nor have ceased to see them.

Sightseeing in London is very hard work in hot weather; especially to thrifty people, who want to compass everything at the least possible expense; who are courageous enough not to want to appear richer than they are; who have no care or fear of whom they may meet; and are determined to see *all* they can in one short week. I still remember a four-mile walk I took with my brother, along Oxford-street to Baker-street, one bright sunny morning, and walking back to our hotel after it.

I was fairly done up; and we had to have a cab in the afternoon to go to Westminster Abbey, where we stayed as long as allowed; never tired of roaming about its grand historic floors, sacred to fame and honour, and saintly and sacred worth. The immortal dead of England are there, if not in their urns, in their effigies, inciting the uplifted eyes of the youth of both sexes, and of all classes and conditions. Our noblest Shakespere was a poor man's child. In fact, the Abbey is a very inspiring place for whoever has a mind to think or a heart to feel.

It is the grandest as well as the holiest spot in the realm, in which every man's rights are equal; the Mecca to which all the sons and daughters of England should make a pilgrimage once in their lives. Our visit there was fruitful in blessed memories, rich in better treasures than knowledge, which have been to me a soul of good amid things evil.

The next day we went by steamboat to Gravesend,

seeing Woolwich and Greenwich; we also visited Chelsea, the latter with its aged pensioners at dinner. We took tea in Cockney fashion, but not with shrimps, for neither George nor I could relish them, having, as my father had, an Erasmian stomach, and a great aversion to all kinds of fish. We were fortunate in not being crowded in the boat, and enjoyed our trip on the river very much.

Returning home at the end of the week, through Oxford, we stayed there a few hours to see something of its glories. Nor were we disappointed in it in so far as we saw, save and except that it seemed somewhat too small and too little imposing for such a noble place. But this is more than forty years ago, and since then the Keble College has been built, and much done beside. And the old place has opened its arms free to England's sons of all sects and denominations, who in return have brought it many honours.

Our visit was very gratifying at home, where father was never tired of asking questions, and hearing us tell him again and again about the wonderful palace of glass. He had never been in London; nor had thousands of the well-to-do men

and women of the middle classes of England of
that time, even in the midland counties; their stay
at home habits having engendered in them, in the
first years of the railway, a singular personal dread
of its dangers.

CHAPTER XIV.

I GREW sadder every day as I grew poorer, refusing to say anything about my wants, but feeling them intensely. In vain my father talked of patience and rest. I was determined to fight for my own living, and be a burden to no one.

At last, in the late autumn—having waited so long, wanting money and many things—I met with an advertisement in the *Baptist Magazine*, and in my despair made up my mind to accept it, if it was at all likely. On scrutinizing it I thought there was something vague about it; but my brother urged me to write to the lady, who lived at Bristol, and make enquiries about it. I did so, which ended in my engaging to go to her.

I went to Bristol in October, but, strange to say, from the first I had a miserable presentiment that in some way—I could not tell how—I should not succeed. I found at once I was in quite a different house to any I had been used to. The lady had but three children; the youngest only about five weeks old. What I was wanted to do or teach, seemed somewhat of a mystery. However, she said we would wait a few days before beginning to do anything. I could do a little sewing in the meantime. I did this, and went out in the middle of the day with the girl—who carried the baby— and the children.

Things were very different to what they had been at Scotby; nothing being stated plainly, but with an amount of reserve. However, I soon learnt a good deal. I learnt that the poor girl was much too hard worked; that she had to leave her work, just in the middle of it, to go out with me and the children; evidently, as it appeared to me, for *show*.

Then again, I found that meals were irregular and meagre, and to say the least, I got very hungry, having often to wait an unmerciful length of time between them. Further, she made a great profession of religion, as a Baptist, and yet I saw she was anxious to make a grand appearance. She put lots of rings and jewellery on before going to speak to her friends, which I did not like. Mrs. Sutton wore no jewels, nor had I any.

I was led to observe, with an aching heart, that a poor washerwoman, who had come to speak to her, was told that her charge was too high, and that she could not pay it. At this the poor woman cried, and said she really could not afford to take them at a less price. That night I was sore vexed I had come to such a house, and knew I could not stay—sham being an abomination in my sight.

I found that the husband was a commercial traveller, seldom or never at home, but on a Sunday; an unpretentious man enough, it seemed to me, who had nothing to do with home affairs, leaving all these to the management of his wife.

However, in such a plight as I found myself, I thought it best to seek an interview with the lady, and frankly ask her to break the engagement. I had now been there more than a week, and nothing was prescribed for me to do. More than this, I perceived she was trying and testing me, as though she had had no testimonials with me. For instance, I found it was left to me to conduct family worship extemporarily, every morning, to see if I could do it, I suppose. I was treated with the utmost distrust, she herself often speaking of the number of Jesuits there were about in society—implying, I thought, that I might possibly be one.

Positively unable to bear it any longer, the next morning I laid before her my request that she would break my engagement and let me go, as I appeared to be doing neither her nor myself any good. To this she at once replied, somewhat fiercely: She should not think of doing so for one moment—said I would get to like Bristol better by and bye; but in that month of fogs such a thing was hardly to be expected! Thus I was put off day after day.

On Friday morning I told her decidedly, as she had refused my wishes, I intended to leave that afternoon for Birmingham. She saw by my manner I could assume a higher attitude than shrinking humility; and every look and word convinced her that I was at last terribly in earnest. She only said, she would write and tell my father. This I knew she would not do, nor did she.

I had but money enough to get to Birmingham, which I reached that November day at twelve o'clock at night. Leaving my luggage at the station, I set out—midnight as it was—to walk through the worse than silent streets. The railway men were very kind, directing me very carefully. When I got to my brother's, I found they were all in bed, but I soon roused them. Their first words were, "Why, we thought you were at Bristol?" And mine, "Let me in, and I will tell you all."

The next day I had ample time to reflect on what I had done, nor could I see cause to regret it, though all was dark and hopeless before me. My father, I knew, fully believed in my doing right (as did my brother and his wife), only regretting that I could not take the more easy way of staying at home.

I began at once to cast about for a situation. I had been corresponding with Mr. J. A. Langford (now Dr. Langford), whom I knew through his being a fellow-contributor to the *People's Journal*, and who, like myself, was then an enthusiastic aspirant after a literary life. To him I had communicated before leaving Bristol, apprising him of my coming; and as he was but a working-man then, on the ground of common equality I sought him out, and found him all I expected—a kind and amiable man, full of hope and cheerful light.

I had done a bold thing, in writing to Mrs. George Dawson, asking her to do me any service in her power. She replied by asking me to call on her at ten o'clock the next day. It was a frosty morning when I set off to Edgbaston to keep the appointment. To me Mrs. Dawson was a very great person, and on the near prospect of seeing her I grew very nervous and shy, so that when I reached the door I could not summon courage to ring the bell. I walked on a considerable distance, promising myself to do it promptly when I came back. At last, in spite of myself, I overcame this foolish diffidence. I found Mrs. Dawson had already gone out, but the servant added, "If you are Miss Smith, I am to be sure to keep you until she returns." So I went in greatly relieved, and sat in the library more than an hour. My long wait had in some measure set me free from my nervousness. The lady's sudden presence, however, almost deprived me of speech, but fortunately she, in her great volubility, made up for my silence.

Seeing my embarrassment, she cut everything short by saying, "Now, we will go upstairs and prepare for dinner. You will talk better after dinner, I know you will." This greatly discomfited me, as I had not come prepared for such a reception. But she would hear of no excuses. She was a lady of much energy and decision, and did her own will as a person not to be denied. She discussed with me all the probabilities of my getting a situation ; and afterwards said she had had a letter from Mr. Osborn of Carlisle (to whom she had written on receiving my note), and he had informed her that they would be glad if I would go back and help them. She wanted me to decide then and there, but on my hesitating to do so, she brought me writing materials and a stamp. Very reluctantly I wrote a few lines to him, and Mrs. Dawson sent it off to the post.

To this letter, in a few days, I received an answer. Mr. Osborn sent a sovereign, and urged me to return at once to them, saying their school had increased, and they would be glad to see me. Knowing that with their large school they must need help, I decided to go back, thinking that as he had sent me a kind letter, they had seen their mistake, and that for the future they would be more appreciative of my services. I thought also that in case the Osborns should not want me, I might stand a better chance of getting a situation in Carlisle. Superstitious, perhaps, I was in my poverty and sorrow; but through all these months of depression, a light beam of hope broke upon me at times, and I more than half believed that an unseen hand was leading me to some home of peace and rest. I was indeed never quite hopeless, though often cast down.

It was on one of the last days of November, 1851, that I left Birmingham to return to Carlisle, with no very elated thoughts, and yet with a feeling that I was not altogether without kind friends. Reaching the old Border city once more, I drove to Castle-street, where the Osborns still lived and had their school. Taking my luggage, the cabman rang the door bell, which was opened, but in a minute was slammed violently to again by the wind. Nobody, neither old nor young, showed face to welcome me. It was a sad omen, and I saw and felt it keenly. Next morning, I was up and busy, taking care to be ready for the school. To my surprise, I was put into a smaller room with the younger children, quite apart from the elder ones and the master. The larger room I was now never invited to enter. There might be various reasons for this course. In the first place, I think he hardly liked me to have an opportunity of observing the progress of the pupils. But little things cropped up that led me to feel certain that progress was more in appearance than in reality.

The younger pupils under me were all better writers than readers, and in many other ways I found the necessary ground work had been neglected. These things, it is true, are getting very much the fashion in our modern schools, public as well as private. The days being dark and short, I was careful to get what I could done in them. As I expected nothing in payment for my services, nor had any kind of privileges in return, I thought I could hardly fail to earn the small pittance I otherwise received in the way of food and lodgings. It was, however, by no means a pleasant position for a person of independent mind. A less shy and timorous person would have contrived at once to "better herself." Alas for me! I thought little in those days of either money or the ordinary affairs of the world. We rubbed on after this fashion until the Christmas holidays, although I saw very clearly that my efforts were looked on with little favour. Still I was inured to that sort of thing, nor did it indeed much discomfit me. I had been invited to come and help them, on account of their having a large school, and plenty to do, which I found true enough.

Altogether I seemed to have been led in a very mysterious way from my home in Oxfordshire, round by Bristol, Birmingham, and back to Carlisle again—almost against my will. The conduct of the lady at Bristol was, to say the least, very strange, and even inexplicable; and not the least strange was it Mr. Osborn's sending me a letter full of an outward show of kindness, and then receiving me so coldly and showing me so much harshness. Still in spite of this I toiled on, perceiving that the prosperity of the school could not possibly last long, unless more arduous and methodical methods were adopted.

When about the first three months had expired— as it drew towards the latter end of February, 1852 —without any hint or forewarning, I received a note from Mr. Osborn one day, telling me without any preface, that I *must* leave their house in a week. Of course it startled and stunned me. How could I get any situation in a week? Or what could I do?

My trouble was extreme. I knew not what to do. I had no money—had been working very hard for them since November, and now it was the first of March, and they had offered me nothing, not even the smallest present. I wept and prayed all the night. I could see no possibility of getting such a situation as I wanted in a few days, or even in a few weeks or months, so I summoned up courage—stung into resolution by unkindness—and resolved to open a school on my own account.

Mr. Osborn said I might do this, on condition that my terms were low, so that I should take no scholars that would be likely to come to them. This I agreed to do, and started the same evening to look for a suitable house. Some of the houses in Dacre-street were at that time nearly finished or building. I took one at the corner rather larger than the rest. This the landlord engaged to have ready in a week. I got a few circulars printed, and distributed them myself, a job not at all to my liking.

CHAPTER XV.

ON the Saturday, when my week was up, I went to my doubly new house. Driven by stress of circumstances, I had to remind my friends of the three pounds they still owed me as the residue of the money I lent them on leaving Westmorland. This I told them I must have absolutely, as well as the furniture of my bedroom, which I had bought on leaving Scotby. These few things, and the three pounds just mentioned, together with five pounds lent me by my brother George, constituted my all when I embarked upon my new venture.

It was a great change to me going into a small house, where I had no one but myself, and a heart full of nothing but fears of failure and disgrace, But I had plenty to do to prepare my little place. I fitted it up myself, and cleaned and brightened everything with my own hands. The work made me cheerful, and sustained me through my troubles as nothing else could.

My little enterprise was to begin on Monday. So on that day I waited and watched and hoped, still finding some little matter to do or improve. At last, when it was getting late, I saw a little girl come to the door and knock. I breathed a prayer for wisdom, and quickly ran to let her in. She told me her simple story, as her mother had bid her, and I cheerfully welcomed her in, and set her by the fire. Suddenly, after a long and dubious pause, another little girl was seen picking her way over the unflagged path. "Is this Miss Smith's school?" she asked. I at once answered "Yes," and set her down with her companion: glad that she had one. I still waited for more pupils, but waited in vain.

Never shall I forget how I longed for the hour when they should leave, that I might give way to the pent up feelings that threatened every now and then to burst forth. However, I had two more in the afternoon, and six or seven before the week end. These increased my hopes; and by the end of the quarter, my little room was over-crowded, and I was obliged to try and get a larger and more convenient place. I was still fearful about doing this, but a friend (the same who had presented me with a new dress) buoyed me up with her hopeful talk.

A house being vacant in West Tower-street, where a Miss Thompson had kept a boarding school, I at once took it; though I did not do this without getting a severe rebuke from Mr. Osborn, who prophesied I would get into debt, ruin myself, and disgrace my friends. This prophecy, I am thankful to say, never came true, for good fortune still attends all who set to work with an earnest determination to do their best.

I was seven years at 11 West Tower-street. It was a busy and somewhat eventful time. I have given a brief glimpse into my inner life, showing myself up most likely as an incomprehensible being. My object has been to show the inner cravings of my soul after literary pursuits, which, being a woman, I failed to attain, despite of all my self-denial and persistent endeavours.

My outer life at school and home was on the whole very prosperous. The knowledge of my tact as a teacher, and the hard life I had led at the other school, had been spread far and wide by the various scholars. My success was now so far established, that to new comers I slightly raised my terms, as I had more rent to pay.

Having no very intimate friends of my own, my heart still clung to the Osborns, and in all their troubles I deemed it my duty, notwithstanding the harsh treatment I had been subject to, to do what I could for them in times of trouble or affliction. Mr. Osborn was a changeable, incautious man. His school did not continue to prosper long. In three or four years he had given it up, and engaged in another and quite different business, so that all their old jealousies towards me had ceased.

But a more serious trouble fell upon their family than I had ever anticipated. In the autumn of the first or second year I was in West Tower-street, a most fatal epidemic of scarletina visited the town of Carlisle, carrying off in a few days whole families, and devastating homes glad with the gay music of childhood, and making them silent. So it had done to the poor and lowly, and it had now come to that of the most learned and pious in the old city —the Reverend Dean Tait, afterwards Archbishop of Canterbury. That sad week when the Dean's children were taken day after day to Stanwix churchyard, Mr. Osborn's were likewise being taken to the cemetery. The Osborns had seven children, one boy and six girls. The eldest—a fair, handsome boy of eleven—was cut off in less than three days. They lost four children in succession by this terrible epidemic. During this trying period I acted in the capacity of sick nurse to them, often sitting up for two or three nights together.

About this time my affairs prospered amazingly. I had to have an assistant teacher; and so full did my school grow that I saw my house was too small to hold all. When I had one scholar from a family I invariably had all the rest, and often the neighbours' children likewise.

Mr. Wingrave, a philanthropic gentleman, who had at that time a night school for young men and women, at the Irish Dam-side, asked me, as he asked other ladies—would I not try and spare a night or two to help him? I agreed to go two nights a week, and did so for a considerable time. Thus I was kept very busy every day in the week; and yet gleams of romance came straying once or twice into my dwelling, where everything was so circumspect and quiet.

Those who have perused my simple story may remember how a little romance had blended with my short period of school life in Westmorland, which through jealousy or some other cause, came to nothing. I had thought nothing more of the affair, nor of any similar affairs. There is no trace of them in what I wrote about this time. I lived for different objects.

And yet I was surprised to learn from Mrs. Osborn, one Saturday morning, that Mr. J——, from Westmorland, was at their house, and was coming to see me. I hardly knew how to receive him. I was engaged with some little household matter when he called. We talked very quietly. He told me he had bought an estate in Ireland, and was then on his way to see it. Of course, I remembered the story he had confided to Mrs. Osborn, as she had also; evidently wishing me to be prepared. But his being rich was counter-balanced by grave eccentricities. Riches were the reverse of attraction to me. I had too independent a mind to allow anyone to say that they had made me rich.

I carried myself with much reserve and circumspection, so as neither by word nor look to make the impression that his attentions would be gratifying to me. Both were grave, as those who had important concerns before them; and in this spirit we bade each other good bye, never again to see one another in this world.

I was not thirty at this time; and a lady, with whom I was well acquainted, was extremely anxious that I should marry her brother. He had a profitable business in the city, of which she was continually telling me, with much praise, but with no success. At last, I received a formal offer of marriage from him. This simply amused me. I got to know that it was not written by himself, as he was nearly blind. It was a pure business transaction that was proposed. It was known I was poor. I never took any pains to conceal it, and a good business was of itself thought a fair prize for an intellectual woman who was struggling with poverty. What an alliance! What presumption!

These things made little impression upon me. I had higher visions than matrimony; literature, poetry, and religion gleamed fair before me. Had I been a young man, how gladly should I have gone into the Nonconformist ministry, and should probably have been accepted. But as a woman I had to struggle with all sorts of difficulties, hardships, and insults; being in the world, but not of it, nor aspiring after any of its flimsy gewgaws.

At West Tower-street, I had two boys who were brothers, one four and the other six, brought to me as boarders. They were the children of my former friend, Miss Jackson of Carlisle, who had married Mr. Harkness of Preston, printer and bookseller. They were with me several years.

Nearly one of the first steps I took in that large house, was to let some of the rooms to a widow woman and her daughter. This was Mrs. Cockbain, an old Baptist friend, whom I greatly respected. I had two or three reasons for doing this. I thought it would be both company and protection for me. Having had great troubles in her married life, she had become a most sincere religious enthusiast. Her lonely prayer, clear-voiced on the midnight, sometimes struck on my absorbed senses as I sat studying less divine, but not less needful things, in my little sitting room; and then beginning very low with her afterwards clearly

chaunted hymn, ever uplifting me and making me
feel blessedly at home. But what power is there
like Religion to sanctify and bless and gladden the
dreariest house, and to bring peace and joy into
the loneliest habitation?

So it was with my old friend. She had little of
what the world boasts of, but she had something
far more precious. She was rich in God's pure
peace and blessing. This homely story may give a
side glance view of a simple scene of which none
was witness but myself. Soon after Mrs. Cockbain
and I had settled down at 11 West Tower-street,
there was to be a public execution at the gaol at
Carlisle. We neither of us believed in public
executions, but our belief was more than mere
negation. I wrote letters to the newspapers, advo-
cating anti-capital punishment views; while my
poor friend (who knew nothing of this) followed
her Bible and the promptings of her own heart,
and had nothing at all to say in defence of her
humane thoughts.

To take a man's life in the open light of day, in
the sight of unreflecting youth and children, seemed
an awful thing to me; and I was determined to

prevent any of my pupils witnessing the shockingly demoralizing scene, which was to take place at noon, when they usually left school. To this end I was walking to and fro, in front of the house, in a spirit of the deepest solemnity. All the time I did this, my friend, who was in her little parlour, was kneeling, with her bonnet and shawl on, at a chair—she had been up the street to see the preparations—and on coming back was so overcome that she had sunk down there. While the bell was tolling, she had been praying, with a voice of the most solemn supplication, for the soul of the condemned man. I always in my heart loved this singularly good woman, because of her sublime sense of real religion.

CHAPTER XVI.

THERE is not much in a struggling life like mine to interest the general reader. From the day I carried my resolution out and stood alone, all things conspired to my prosperity. I spoke to no one about it, but by the kind sympathizing looks and words I met everywhere, everyone seemed to know —and I really think they did in some mysterious way—so fully aware did they seem to be of the hard struggle I had had to do right.

But in the cross I had voluntarily taken, I felt divine strength. My feet were firm, and if I had no very brilliant hopes, neither had I any certain fears. A mystic by nature, loneliness made me much more so now, and there were things at times that were unaccountable to me. Here is one which long lay secret in my own heart, and not till many years after its occurrence, became what we call true. One day, suddenly, a certain passage I could not remember reading before persistently followed me, and presented itself to my mind. Over and over again it did this, as a solemn song in my soul, till at last I was obliged to take notice of it in its endless occurrence to my mind. "And those that afflicted thee, shall come bending unto thee, and thine enemies shall lick the dust; and thy wings shall be covered with silver, and thy feathers with yellow gold."

This poetic passage of scripture was part of it fulfilled before many months were over, and the latter and more hyperbolical part in a way eventually. I was, as will be seen, like all religious people, very superstitious, and still am so. To another, all this would be false; to me it was a mysterious truth that the years have never dimmed nor darkened. Among other things it helped to comfort and strengthen my heart in my many trials, and gave me courage to hope in the future.

My school increased more and more, for if I lost my best scholars, I had still new ones brought. So I worked on, little disconcerted by my difficulties, nor was my life unhappy. I had no debts. My work was my comfort; and the few friends who called to pay their bills were warm in their thanks and praise. With my increasing school, I had to have a permanent assistant. My two boy boarders necessitated this. I no longer let any part of my house, but filled it all with busy life.

My terms were so very low, that hard as I worked, I did little more than pay the most economical household expenses. My dread of debt was worse than anything else, sometimes casting me down very low; and yet I had not courage to raise my terms, nor did I see how I could do so without endangering my school. Yet fearing many things, I contrived to save a little, spending nothing on fine dress or furniture, I kept none but the plainest company. One or two poet friends— working men—who occasionally called to see me on a Sunday; religion and poetry being the subject of their talk, or the last new book, or the reviews.

The cotton famine and the American war of emancipation occurred at this time, which afforded constant matter for interesting conversation in every circle. In England there were two parties, north and south; those who stood for property, and those who stood for right. I stood for what I thought was the right. I had been brought up in the air of freedom by my Nonconformist father; and wherever a voice breathed a prayer, or song, or shout of liberty, it thrilled through my very soul. I remember well, when very young, hearing the Rev. Eustace Carey preach, and in his enthusiasm crying out: "Proud America! Boasting America! with thy Stars and Stripes! And yet it waves in mockery over three million slaves!"

It was a chapter and a sermon; and yet the great human heart that listened, out of its deep silences, burst forth in loud bravos. From that hour slavery appeared to me as one of the curses of the world. So I fully knew my mind on this occasion.

We had had the Crimean war before this time, with which I had little sympathy. I have always had the singular faculty, for a woman, of forming my own judgment on such things. It was a great quarrel among kings, fought out for their good, at the expense of the common people. A wise and just man, like Oliver Cromwell, would have sent the whole lot of them to the right about.

But with other ladies in Carlisle, and other towns of England, I felt much for the poor soldiers, the victims of this cruel war. Along with my elder pupils, I set to work to minister to their comfort. My little parlour was filled with busy people for many weeks during the late autumn evenings. To the aid and sustenance of these men, Florence Nightingale, one of the noblest ladies in England, had gone forth.

So we worked and talked, with many hundreds of Englishwomen, in those dark days; collecting the money first to buy wool and worsted, flannel and warm calicoes, which we made into shirts and drawers, or knit into mufflers, stockings, gloves, socks, and all sorts of useful things. With glowing hearts, these were packed into large packages, and sent off with others which went from Carlisle to the 'far off battle field.

About this time I made the acquaintance of a singularly enthusiastic orator, Mr. Washington Wilks, who was living at Blackwell House, near Carlisle. He came to the town as editor of the *Carlisle Journal*, but holding views too advanced for the organ of the old Whig party, he became the first editor of a new local venture, the *Carlisle Examiner*. He had been on the staff of the *Morning Star*, a London radical and democratic paper. I first met him at one of the popular Saturday night lectures, which he instituted for working men, and where he attracted great crowds of hearers.

Soon after Mr. Wilks came to the old city, there was a parliamentary election, and at such times there usually was a great deal of bitter resentful language used on both sides. Squibs of all kinds were flying about; and persons' faults and peculiarities occasionally were cruelly pressed into the service of politics. I protested against this as wrong; and Mr. Wilks and Dr. Evans agreeing with me, invited me to help them to bring out a small tract against it, while the election lasted.

I very willingly agreed to do this, writing short tales illustrative of what was wanted, scraps of conciliatory verse, etc. This plan we carried out, issuing our little tracts anonymously, mostly at intervals of two or three days, at our own expense, and giving them away wherever acceptable. Our object was to induce all parties to use more courteous speech, and observe more christian feeling in their political agitations. But the old noisy spirit and feeling prevailed very much at that time in the city.

In every assembly for the discussion or settlement of business, very strong language was the rule, and citizens did not fail to hear very graphically of all their faults and offences, known or unknown. Very grotesque epithets were often applied to upright and respectable men, merely to create a laugh; but woe to him whose character would not bear public inspection! To such an one, all his private misdeeds suddenly became public ones, caricatured twenty-fold.

So it was in the Town Council, as often as it met. To the northerners it only excited a laugh; but to people like Mr. Wilks and myself, and others from the south, it was a thing to be deeply deplored, and silently discouraged, if by no other means. An editor who came to Carlisle from London about this time, once said to me, "Do you ever read the Town Council proceedings, Miss Smith? Isn't it awful!" And surely it was. We felt that at this election time, it would be wise to attempt something, at least, in the right direction. It bore some fruit, for many of the *elite* of the working men, as well as the religious community, took it up and cultivated it in their meetings.

Mr. Wilks' influence and spirit, during the three or four years he was in Carlisle, had a very salutary effect on the aspiring working men of the old city. In all towns, their better life and tendency, both in religion and politics, often receives its impetus from some one or two men who through ability and example are constituted their leaders.

Mr. Osborn had before this gathered the working men to his classes, and led them to feel the worth of self-respect and the value of education, by producing for them his "Short Grammar" and "Handbook of Logic." They joined his class in great numbers, in the Independent school-rooms, Lowther-street. They learned much from him, which led them to thoughtful, studious habits, not readers only, but men who could think and decide a point for themselves. Mr. Osborn, poor man! might perhaps have been better thought of in Carlisle—for he certainly did much good there— had it not been for the instability of his character.

From the first, Mr. Wilks delivered Saturday night lectures in the Shaddongate school-room, free of charge, which attracted crowded audiences, for a considerable time. He was a thinker as well as an eloquent speaker, and was author of "The Latter Half of the Nineteenth Century." Best of all, he was a man of an eminently religious spirit, and could preach an eloquent sermon. His lectures and newspaper articles, though often ultra radical, were invariably very inspiring.

He fraternized very freely with the working-men, esteeming himself one of them. He was always ready to do them any good in his power; and they, on their part, believed in him with an implicit faith, so that long after he had left Carlisle, a report of his coming would bring a great crowd to hear him. It was at these lectures I met many of the *elite* of the working men, such as Thomas Hardy, James Walker, Robert Wales, and others.

I got more settled and reconciled to my way of life, filling it completely with various labours which were constantly in hands. I helped Lonsdale with his *Observer*, writing at that time under the *nom de plume* of "Mary Osborn." It was while looking over the gardens at the back of Fisher-street, in May, that I wrote, "May Musings," which was published in the *Observer*.

While in West Tower-street I was very assiduous

with my German, having my books always handy to fill up any vacant interval of time. Such was my ardour, that I soon achieved a fair amount of success, so far as Schiller's plays and poetry were concerned. The idiom of Goethe's writings, I found less to my liking. Nor did I think favourably of the style and spirit of his works, which I never could induce myself to admire. I always fancied him devoid of veneration, though I admit there are fine passages in Wilhelm Meister, otherwise I think he has done more than any other writer to introduce that spirit of secularism that now so extensively prevails in literature and amongst literary people.

I was soon able to read and enjoy Schiller, and as I took care to get his plays in German, they were taken about with me wherever I went. In learning it, I had little idea of ever teaching it; nor did I but once try to do so, and then it was to help an orphan boy, and so save the expense of his getting a master.

I had now been seven years in West Tower-street, having gone there in 1852. Year by year my school had gone on increasing, till the place was really too small for it. It was here it developed largely into a school for the education of farmers' daughters and others, whose parents saw them on the verge of womanhood with very little knowledge or in almost total ignorance. These hearing of me as one who took much pains with dunces and the neglected, sent their children to me a few quarters to get a bit of education. I tried to interest them in it so far as to make them see and feel that it was a delightful thing, and quite worth all the pains and trouble bestowed upon it. I tried to impress upon them, that a young woman without education had been sadly wronged and injured, but that with it she had opportunities of rising higher in society than by any other means.

My pupils from the first were struck with my simple ways and the absence of tuitional hauteur, and my odd ways, "like a mother," of telling them bits of things in explanation of the life and nature around them. So that some tiny boy or girl interested father and mother very much at dinner by telling them what I had said that morning about insect or animal life, or why we should have the windows open and our skins quite clean. The old methods were never altogether mine. I believed with deep reverence in the Bible of Nature, as well as that of Moses and the Prophets.

My house, in a great measure, now became pleasant to me. I had no critics to interfere with my doings; and though I felt my isolation very much at times, I contrived to fill my life with all sorts of work, both for myself and others. My school, of course, was always my first and foremost object. I made it a rule from the beginning that I was only to be called out of it by those who wanted me respecting it. Others must see me at some other time. This rule I kept all through the years I had a school. But my terms—principally through Mr. Osborn's interference—were exceedingly low, and having no help nor capital to begin with, I was kept very poor.

But I was not without annoyances and vexations. After good Mrs. Cockbain left, she had recommended me to a Scotchwoman, a Presbyterian and a widow, the mother of two growing youths. The boys were clerks in lawyers' offices, steady blameless young men. The mother could talk a good deal, especially about her religion. She was a very regular attendant on Sundays, and consequently beguiled me into believing her words and accepting her as Mrs. Cockbain's successor.

This universal belief in people often brought me into trouble, placed as I was among strangers. It did so in this case. I soon found her talk was a froth of falsity, which I hated; that she neglected every home duty; put her best things on in a morning, and went out gossipping, leaving her poor boys to come home to their dinner, when there was neither food nor fire for them. More than that, instead of paying at the week end, she told me fine stories of a rich Scotch uncle, who was coming to see her and bring her money, but who never did come.

I was easy with her at the first, and being surrounded with trouble at the time, she got three or four pounds in my debt before I was able to take any steps about it. I felt she must leave, and told her so; and told her also that her furniture, which I found she was selling, must be left until she had paid what she owed me.

I went to Fisher-street at the Whitsuntide Term, 1859. The sun shone brightly as we packed the large cart, which came for the furniture at four o'clock in the morning. I loved privacy, and had an idea of getting all away soon after six. I was determined to go on as I had begun, without any pretence, or show, or display of any kind. The years I had just ended in Tower-street had been prosperous ones, through hard work and economy. I left much richer than I came. I bought additional furniture while there, paying for it when got, for I carried out my principle of owing no man any thing.

Life was getting very busy and full of responsibility to me. In going through Preston to Oxfordshire, I stopped a few days with Mr. Harkness, the father of two of my scholars. He was a printer, and took me over his works, telling me all about them. I told him I had a large number of occasional poems, which I had some thoughts of getting printed at some future time, when I could afford it. I thought privately it was perhaps my duty to return something back in this way, for what I had been paid for his boys' schooling.

So without much thought or reflection, we concluded our bargain. When they came to hand, the books distressed and tried me very much. In every way they were such as I could take no pleasure in. I had the feeling that the bill for them must be paid before I could ever have a bit of rest. Truly I watered my pillow with tears. It took all the sense of vanity out of me. I don't think I realized a single pound by the transaction.

I took no interest at all in the volume; hardly thought it right to offer it for sale, though I knew that no one need be ashamed of the most part of the poems it contained. Thomas Carlyle and his wife had commended them as full of thought, and one of the pieces as like *singing*; but to promote the sale of them by any means, with so many imperfections, I never could—nor did—do.

However, one thing occurred, which comforted me very much, though I only named it to a few intimate friends. An excellent review of the book appeared in the *Carlisle Journal*. A young man, sub-editor at the time, I was told was the writer of it. It was no petty partial praise, but was full and hearty.

But I had sunk very low in spirits, and the few friends who spoke highly of them, found me in no mood to be flattered. Mr. Wilks was leaving

Carlisle. In his last lecture at Shaddongate, he referred to my poems, praised them very much, and quoted some stanzas from the one entitled "Opportunity."

> Doubt and gloom and needless sorrow,
> Have no need the mind to gloom ;
> What comes not to-day, to-morrow
> Will on golden pinions come.
> Come as comes the light of morning,
> Come as come the stars of night,
> Come God's visits without warning,
> Crowning life with glory bright.

I gave away many copies of my volume. In about a year's time I got the whole bill paid, after which I managed to get the annoyance of it off my mind, but not till then.

My greatest grief was that the only eyes which would have looked kindly on my verses were those of my dear father, and they were closed in death before the volume appeared. I, who loved him so much, had a nice plain white stone put at his grave, choosing, for my own gratification, to do all at my own expense. That stone is still standing, with two lines of my own on it, in Cropredy churchyard.

CHAPTER XVII.

OWING to the circumstance of my house in Fisher-street being wanted for some particular purpose, I was obliged to look out for an abode for myself, and a school-room for my pupils. Driven to decide, I succeeded in taking a place in Finkle-street, a large roomy house, with a snug plot of open ground behind. It was not by any means a fashionable house, nor was it situated in a fashionable street, and yet the neighbourhood was a highly respectable one. Immediately in front, the old Friends' burial ground, planted with lilacs and laburnums, made it a perfect paradise of beauty and fragrance in spring time.

Altogether this was the best house I ever occupied. I was not likely to feel anything like being cramped in it. Dr. Elliott, calling on me for some purpose one Saturday evening, when I happened to be out, went with my girl over the house and backyard, all of the rooms of which were carefully cleaned every week.   He left word that he was very much pleased with what he had seen; that it was very healthy, and was quite fit for a school. Hence I could speak with confidence to that effect, when anxious mothers brought delicate children to me.

I went to the house in Finkle-street at Whitsuntide, 1861, occupying it as long as I was able to conduct a school.   I afterwards lived in it in my private capacity for another year, and then left for the south.

It was while at this house that I began regularly those long walks for my health, along the Brampton road, by Whiteclosegate, and often in the delightful summer nights as far as Brunstock bridge, to have a contemplative sit there, in near vision of Drawdykes castle and its lively country life.   Or on a lovely summer Sunday, round by Linstock and Rickerby—a delightful walk for any lover of nature. Many a line have I composed there "far from the madding crowd."

I often thought the view looking over Carlisle in the direction of West Cumberland, from the rising ground at Whiteclosegate, very fine, almost finer than anything else in the neighbourhood. Going from Whiteclosegate to Brunstock bridge, you descend one of the most beautiful broad roads I have seen in the north. It is like those of my native county, well set with trees on both sides, and high banked with an abundance of lovely wild flowers.

I have got there abundantly on summer evenings, handfuls of fragrant wild woodbine; and there, and there only, as in my native wanderings, have I heard the merry cuckoo sounding its own name from the far woodlands. This road is a remarkably rural one. Hence I adopted it as one for my constant walk; and I seemed to enjoy it all the more when I got used to it. And if, as often happened, I was told I met friends, looked them in the face, and yet did not see them, they excused me, knowing that I had lost myself, or that the spell of some poetic dream had seized me.

Coming back one Sunday afternoon in summer with a poet friend to whom I could express my admiration only by a gesture now and then, as he was quite deaf, he said as we neared Rickerby, "I lose a great deal now, I see, by not being able to hear your talk at such a time as this." I simply bowed a mute assent, knowing that he also felt the great spirit that had taken possession of me.

Was it this great spirit that took possession of the mind of Christ on the hills of Judea? or of other divine men in other parts of the world? Anywise, we might cultivate the blessed solitudes of nature with much advantage to our spiritual experiences. In getting and spending, we truly lay waste our lives; nor does money compensate us for the grandeurs we rob ourselves of thereby.

We need to read the American stoic, Emerson, and learn what divine strength there is in nature, and how poor we are, isolated from her in towns. Whenever I was going to read or speak, in the after time, I always tried to get a walk up my favourite road before doing so. But he will understand little of the blessed secrets of nature who goes off to his communion with a heart devoid of prayer. He must absolve himself to her, and breathe her pure breath; give himself to a great purpose, and she will help him as she only can.

Mr. Joseph Hannah, who at that time had a large prosperous mixed school in Carlisle, an excellent teacher and a sensible man—though I never had the advantage of his acquaintance—I heard spoke very well of me as a teacher. A great many of my pupils had in the course of time come under him, and he had found them well forward, especially in all the first branches of learning. I was told he would often set any new pupil who had been at my school up to read a poem to him, just to hear how well he could do it. This implied that the little head, young as it was, knew all about it, and could understand the poetry as well as read it. When enthusiasts teach, children will soon learn.

Mr. Hannah often remarked to parents that they could not do better than let their children stop with me. I was very grateful to him, as I ought to be, for saying it. And let me say it, he had nothing to get by being generous to me.

Many of my boys also went to the Grammar School. So early as when Mr. Durham was head master, this was the case. A gentleman, whose two boys went there, told me that the first morning one of them was there, the second master was struck with the good writing of the new scholar. He forthwith took it up to Mr. Durham, who sent for his eleven year old pupil, and said to him, "Who taught you to write, my boy?" The reply was, "Miss Smith, if you please, sir." Mr. Durham said, "Miss Smith knows how to teach boys to write."

I merely state this to show that I taught, or attempted to do so, thoroughly well. The eyes of little boys often twinkled when they came up to me with their first copies. Whenever I could praise, I did so heartily. "Why, this is really capital! You'll soon be a good writer: one of the best in the school, I can see." No cane in Christendom could have wrought the magic those few words did.

Approach them the right way, children like to learn, though you may have failed to learn what. I once had a little fellow, restless and idle. I could not find out anything he would do in the way of work. One day there was a clear outline of a beautiful bird on a copybook back lying on the desk. Seeing it, I involuntarily said, as I held it up for all to see, "I wonder who could draw me this?" All were silent; but by and bye, I saw my little restless friend kneeling up to the desk, slate and pencil in hand. He soon drew a very accurate outline of the bird, and having done so, left his slate on the desk for me to see, being too shy to bring it up.

But I was observant, and seeing all eyes turned to Joseph's slate, I also went to examine it. For a child who had never begun to draw, it was wonderful; indeed, all the school wondered. I saw he was watching my face to see, rather than hear, what I would say. I turned to him with a kindly smile, and said: "Now, Joseph, I have found out what you can do well; better than any of us." And yet it came to pass that the boy never accomplished anything in an artistic line. His father, a prosperous man of business—to whom I sent word that Joseph might become a successful painter—I was led to understand had no higher aim of the thing than sign painting. And the little fellow was soon after sent to another school, perhaps as a result of my communication.

In the first quarter of my school life, I had helped Mr. Wingrave with an evening class of poor girls, of about fifteen or sixteen, at the Irish-damside. They were for the most part street vendors of yellow

clay. Other ladies also assisted occasionally. These
girls learnt much by association, as well as by their
books and slates. Many were shy, modest girls,
ashamed to say they could not read, till I, whispering
to them, invited them into some corner, and tried
to teach them. A number thus learnt to read and
write a little in a short time, very proud of their
progress.

This class was held in a large old room of what
had once been a dwelling house, approached by a
lobby upstairs. Being situated in a low neighbourhood, rough boys with sticks came every night and
rattled at the door. Mr. Wingrave was out one
night, and as we had only a very young man in the
room, we were somewhat afraid. However, I went
to the door, and called to a big bare-headed boy,
with a great stick in his hand, "It's Dan I want."
He at once came. I knew him to be the worst of
the gang; but I said, "Now, Dan, as Mr. Wingrave
is away, I want you to stand at the door here, and
keep those rough boys away."

He showed his Irish nature by a fine bow, and a
"Yes, ma'am;" and he kept the door effectually,
save that I once had to go out and ask him not to

hurt any one, as I feared he was doing. From that time he came every night to his post. We invited him in, gave him a book, and if he got nothing else, he got a little civilization.

Two or three years after, as my pupils went out in the morning at West Tower-street, one of them ran back to tell me, with some surprise, that some one wanted to speak to me at the door. It was my old acquaintance, Dan, cleanly washed and dressed, with a basket on his arm, and a bag on his back. He had plates and dishes in his basket, and bones, I suppose, in his bag.

I exclaimed, "Why, Dan, is that you?" With the old smile and bow, "Yes, ma'am," he replied. I asked after his sister, one of the best in the school, who had not been able to read before attending there. He said she had got a place now, and told me other things, but never once asked me to buy. "Now I know where you live, ma'am, I am glad," was his final salutation. Poor Dan! his cleanly courteous Irish face has been one I have ever remembered with gratitude.

> But knowledge to their eyes her ample page,
> Rich with the spoils of time, did ne'er unroll;
> Chill penury repressed their noble rage,
> And froze the genial current of the soul.

I had a deep longing at this time to do some good in the world. I hardly knew what. My ambition had been from an early period to write books; but my hard work and added years (for I was now getting up to forty) had taught me that for this, like many other things, I had no means to carry out such an object, but must follow patiently the harder and narrower fortunes of meaner women. But I was resolved to do what I could, and to do that in a right spirit, never making gain my sole and only aim.

So when I was asked to help in an evening school for factory girls, carried on at that time by the Carrs, I very willingly agreed to do so. Mr. James Carr said if I could go four nights a week, they could have a double school; that is, one set of girls coming the first two nights, and another set the next two. To this I consented, and the idea was carried out. Other ladies attended, though no one but myself went more than two nights a week. I did full duty there for more than a year. At that time I had a very trustworthy girl I could leave at home, to take care of my house. The coming and going to and from Caldewgate, where the school was held, was trying to me on wet and wintry nights.

It was about this time that I first began to give little sketches in the newspapers. I sent many things of this sort to the *Carlisle Express*, which they were always glad to receive. The Rev. W. J. Tweddle came to preach the anniversary sermons at the Fisher-street Wesleyan chapel for many years. These sermons were often very badly reported in the newspapers. Knowing me to have a gift for such work, Mr. Tweddle once said, "Miss Smith, they do make such work with my sermons. I wish you would take them in hand."

From that time I did so, and they generally filled a column in the *Express*. I also reported the sermons of the Rev. W. R. Percival in *extenso* for the same paper.

But I had had a yet harder task to do in this way, some years before, when the *Carlisle Examiner* was in the hands of Mr. Tuck, on the West-walls. Dean Close, soon after coming to Carlisle, gave two lectures exclusively to women; not a man was to be admitted, not even a reporter. And this rule was rigidly enforced.

In this extremity, Tuck sent to me—would I kindly go to the meeting, and send them a report? so his note ran. I replied I would see what I could do; but the lecture was that night, and I had not got a ticket. I sent everywhere, but could not get one. What was I to do? Try a kind word. The place was full when I went. I said to the man who stood at the door, to put people in their seats, "Please let me in. I have no ticket, but I have an object in view." He let me in without demur, taking me down—it was in the old Athenæum—to the bottom seat close to the platform.

Presently the dean came in by himself, and mounted the platform, looking round as he did so on his full audience of women, and saying in a jubilant voice, "Now we have none of those reporters here to-night, and we can say what we like." He could have laid his hand on my head, so near was I to him. I said to myself, "Wait a wee, good master dean. I am here to do what I can." I followed him closely for two hours till he had done. I then posted home, sent my boarders to bed, and finished my report before I went myself.

To the surprise of all—the dean the most of all—the report appeared in the paper the next morning, and at the top of it was the announcement, "From our Lady Reporter." I did not agree to this. But nobody believed it was a woman, not even the dean, though he accepted the report, and sent copies of it to his friends.

When he came to the next lecture, he said he believed a man in woman's clothes had been there and reported it. At this meeting, which was a fortnight after the first, I was there half an hour before the time. I found to my dismay the place was quite full, and the doors were shut. No more were to be admitted, although there was a hundred or two outside. I was at a loss to know what to do. But a thought struck me that I might get in with the dean when he came. Had the dean come? I asked, and found not.

So I started off down Lowther-street, to meet him. I soon saw his giant-like figure coming along, with a great staff in his hand. He was quite alone, and I walked quietly a little behind him on one side. As many people were about, no one noticed it. When we came to the door the dean gave it a hearty rap, and everybody gave way to him. Keeping a steadfast step by him, I went in unobserved by his side. No one conceived that I did not belong to him. Once in, I hastened to get forward into the hall. Two girls were taking tickets, and they demurred to letting me pass; but leaving my ticket with one of them, I sprang forward. I saw clear enough that I should have to stand, and did so for nearly two hours—all the time the lecture lasted.

This time, when the dean came on the platform, he ran his eye round the vast audience, looking, as it were, to see if he could detect this man in woman's clothes, who calls himself "Our Lady Reporter." In the interval everyone scrutinized her neighbour, and I, of course, to avoid observation, did as the rest did. This was repeated more than once during the lecture, so he seemed to be bent on finding the "man in woman's clothes."

But I stood firm, and his second lecture, as the first, duly appeared, filling nearly two columns of the *Examiner*, of which he confessed he bought many to send to his friends. How I did this seemingly impossible and wholly gratuitous work may seem strange, but it is not new, as some reporters have used the self-same method. I had neither pencil nor paper; did everything with my memory alone; my way being to catch the salient points or heads, making them firm as the lecture proceeded, by the illustrations used, or by any peculiarity of speech or idea, or any singular phrase.

With these "heads" following on consecutively, when I sat down to write my lecture out, I always found it easy to fill in the details, hardly ever once getting lost, or not being able to keep on writing as fast as I could.

CHAPTER XVIII.

A DEAR friend, who had much influence over me, some years after this, was the Rev. W. R. Percival, who came to Carlisle to assist Dean Close in some of the poorer districts of the town. He was a man of much thought, and capable of much spiritual elevation and enthusiasm; of a very gentle loving disposition and beautiful manners. These had the effect of endearing him to all classes and conditions of people.

I was first introduced to him at a large soiree of working men, held in Shaddongate, by Mr. Wilks, where they were both to speak. I was struck with his catholic spirit and bearing, for he was pre-eminently a christian minister and a religious man, having scarcely anything of the politician about him, yet that night he spoke on christian co-operation. Mr. Wilks and he—although as far as the poles asunder—had something in common, being both christian men, and greatly desirous of uplifting the masses.

Mr. Percival had been some months in Carlisle before I had an opportunity of seeing or hearing him, or indeed before he was known at all out of church circles. Then a report of Dean Close having used him harshly flew over the old city, and all but the narrowest sectarians sympathized with him and his young family. He had occupied the position of one of the teachers at the Cheltenham Training College for Teachers, and had been for some time seeking holy orders in the Church of England.

Dean Close had met with him, and had been struck with the grasp of his mind, and his gentle manly bearing. Knowing his wishes, he offered him a curacy under him at Carlisle. The two got on well for some time, but then it was said that the people ran after the dean's curate more than they did after the dean.

Mr. Percival's faults all came to the surface. He was charged, as many good men have been, with heterodoxy. This he was from certain standpoints, but had at first stated he was a follower of Frederick

Denison Maurice, who was in the Church, as were thousands of others holding the same belief. However, poor Percival was summoned to Rose-castle, to be questioned by Bishop Waldegrave, an extreme low churchman, which course ended in his being asked to resign the post he held.

He was urged to form a church on Congregational principles, in the hall of the Mechanics' Institute, which he did, and preached there for a number of years his own peculiar doctrines, which were those of the Broad Church school. He used to say that he had all the best heads in Carlisle, and truly at one time I think he had. The first Sunday he preached in the Mechanics' Hall, I went to report his sermons, as promised. As I was not rich to contribute to the funds, I was very glad to help in this way, using my memory solely, without any help of pencil at all.

Lonsdale, whom I helped occasionally with his newspaper, favoured me in return by the insertion of anything I sent. I sent very full accounts of the opening services, when Mr. Percival began, which probably helped a little to fill the place. It was a wonder to many how his sermons got so often in the papers, as no reporter was ever seen there. The secret was only known to myself and a few others.

I had in Mr. Percival and his wife very congenial friends as long as they were in Carlisle. I attended his church regularly, and even became a member. He had had a great disappointment, and was still anxious to get into the Church of England, in which he certainly seemed to have a good prospect of rising. But there are narrow orthodox spirits everywhere, and perhaps more so in cathedral towns. This class counted his good as evil, and in some cases bore false witness against him. He was a deeply injured man, and his fine capacities were, to a certain extent, crushed out. Such things were the means of depressing and almost driving him to madness. During the last year or two he was in Carlisle, I was often fearful of some tragic occurrence, which, thank God, never occurred.

At length, persuaded to think of his own and his family's good, he left for London, where he preached to crowded congregations in Newman Hall's chapel and other places. Finally, he got ordination in the church of his choice, and became one of the coworkers with the Rev. J. Lambert in London, where, after some years of hard parochial labour, he laid down his life, as many another true and faithful servant of Christ has done.

In telling the story of this good man, I must not omit to state that he met with one generous friend in Carlisle, in the person of Mr. John Clark Ferguson, who attended his ministry. Besides subscribing liberally to the church in Carlisle, after they got to London he allowed them a hundred pounds a year. I believe this sum was also continued to Mrs. Percival, when she became a widow, an act of true christianity worthy of the generous family from whom it originated. There were many others, of more limited means than Mr. Ferguson, who stood firmly by Mr. Percival in his many trials.

When will the world learn that the heterodoxy of one age is the orthodoxy of the next? Christ did not come into the world to condemn it. Are we greater than He?

Here is an anecdote of Mr. Percival, told me by a gentleman at whose house he had been taking tea, and who was walking along English-street with him on his way home. It was between nine and ten o'clock, and the streets happened to be crowded with people.   At one place they were much jostled, and Mr. Percival was awkwardly pushed against a street girl.   He expressed great sorrow, and proposed to go back and beg her pardon.   His friend remonstrated, as it had been done accidentally.   But back he went, and with hat in hand begged her pardon.   The poor girl could not understand the drift of it at first, but seeing his serious looks, burst into tears, and exclaimed: "O Lord, don't beg my pardon!"

This simple act roused her more than anything else could have done, perhaps, to a sense of her own true humanity from which she had fallen. When Mr. Percival returned to his friend, with a satisfied look, he resumed the thread of the conversation as if nothing had happened.

I perhaps may say here that now in age and pain, and in the daily expectation of deliverance from this body of sin and death, I remain very much in my spiritual beliefs as many years ago when I joined Mr. Percival's church, save that I was then, and have all my life been, more of a Nonconformist than he was.   My great devotion to Emerson made, for many years, a deep impression on some of my religious ideas. But in the presence of the great realities of death, and in the sight of God, the soul, in prayer and self-examination, sees things more humbly and rightly; sees, indeed, the surpassing need we have of Christ, as our spiritual guide, light, life, and way; sees how He is our Saviour.

I have all my life disliked controversy, as did my father. Still he used to say, "If it is calculated to do good, let it go on." I have said, and still say the same. This view of it is based on the sermon on the mount, and accords with the deepest humility which Christ taught. Truly, we ought to be more like Him in all things. What we believe is not of so much importance as what we are.

I began to read in public soon after I went to live in Finkle-street. I had a large school; worked very hard in the day, and often had private pupils in the evening; so fearful was I that I should not be able to pay the rent of my large house. I had also an additional boarder, a young lady of seventeen, a ward in chancery. I took great pains to make my pupils read naturally and effectually;—a rarer gift than music, as I often told them.

My first reading in public was by no means my own choosing. A young dissenting minister had made an engagement with the committee connected with Shaddongate school-room, to lecture for them on a certain Saturday night. Something prevented him from keeping his promise; and not knowing what to do, they came and asked me if I could help them out of their difficulty. When I arrived on the scene, every inch of space in that large room was crowded out, some were standing outside, and I had a difficulty to get in. Mrs. Fisher was in the chair, and introduced me.

As I had received such short notice, I read what I felt sure I could read the best. I only know now that I read Macaulay's "Armada," one of Owen Meredith's poems, and Tennyson's "May Queen." Every one was well received; and the "May Queen" had a most appreciative and delightful reception. I believe it had never been read publicly in Carlisle before. I could hardly get on for applause. Mr. Percival was there, and afterwards urged me to give readings in connection with his church.

But it was not till the following autumn that I began the "Penny Readings" in Carlisle. The following is their simple history. I went into Oxfordshire at midsummer, as I had usually done for a number of years. I met the local Baptist minister, the Rev. W. Henderson, now of London, at my brother's. He was an intellectual man, and among other things, he told me of the success that had attended some readings. Many who would not go near the chapel on Sunday, came to the readings on the week nights. The place was crowded with coal-heavers, washerwomen, and all sorts of people, a penny entrance being charged to help to defray expenses.

I saw that such readings as these might do good in Carlisle. Accordingly when I got settled at home in the autumn, I began to cast about how I could best bring my idea into practical effect. I talked to my friends about it, and among others to Mr. Percival. He warmly approved of the idea, and told me that William Holstead, who was an excellent reader, and others, had been holding readings in connection with his church while I was in Oxfordshire.

One Sunday morning in October, after attending Mr. Percival's service, Mr. Holstead walked down Lowther-street with me to the foot of Rickergate. I had spoken to him before about the readings, and now again took the opportunity to say emphatically that if they were managed with decent tact and economy they would certainly succeed. Nothing would convince him, although he was willing to help in any way he could. My ideas seemed to be too large for him, and he did little more than pull his moustache and express his doubts.

At last, he agreed to my proposal that we should try it for three weeks, the readings to take place on the Monday or Saturday nights. Our first meeting was on a Saturday night, and Dr. Elliot was in the chair. It was not a success, but success could not come at once. We then changed to Monday night. The second meeting was better; and on the third night the room was crowded to the door, with numbers standing outside.

All through the first winter there was no falling

off in the attendance; and on some occasions of particular interest, the penny tickets were re-sold at six and even nine times their original cost. Mr. Holstead and Mr. Robert Lattimer were the most popular readers, but there were others—such as the Rev. J. Tasker and Mr. Gosling of the County hotel—who were very much appreciated. When the days began to lengthen, we gave them up for that season.

Thus the first winter's meetings closed with eminent success, and with the commendation of the whole community. Mr. Holstead had worked indefatigably, having had the management of the business part of the matter in his own hands—no small affair. After all expenses had been paid, there was a surplus of twenty-seven pounds left. Five pounds of this was sent to the Dispensary, and the remaining twenty odd pounds was expended upon free beds for the House of Recovery. This was a great consolation. We felt that our efforts and anxieties had not been in vain. This season's readings were the first and last that I had to do with, as I had the misfortune to fall ill of a fever the next September, which left me weak and feeble for twelve months after.

CHAPTER XIX.

POETRY indeed was through all the hard periods of my life, my joy and strength, the uplifter of my soul in trouble. Now it was that every prospect of a literary career—always the cherished ideal of my soul—seemed forever blocked out of my prospects and hopes. I, who would cheerfully have gone ragged and barefoot to have had the meanest place in the temple of lofty learning, was now, by my very success as a teacher, and with my own hand, bolting the door of my own higher hopes on my soul.

Never were these things spoken of to others. Had I done so, I knew the kindest friend would have thought me somewhat demented. Indeed, so strong my feelings grew about this time on this subject, that the prosperity of my school rather depressed than gladdened me. Urged on by these feelings, in spite of my natural timidity, after much thought, I conceived the bold idea of writing to Mrs. Carlyle of Chelsea, telling her the state of my mind and asking her advice.

I hardly expected an answer, when, lo! in a few mornings the postman brought me a small envelope, with a narrow edging of black, containing a letter from Mrs. Carlyle.*　When I saw who it was from, I was too overpowered for some time to read it, but when I did so I at once fell in love with this dear woman, who ever after was one of the greatest idols of my heart.　Her letters to me advised patience, and, in one of them, she praised a little poem I had sent, entitled "The Present."　In her own phraseology, "Thomas, to whom she had read it—who rarely praised poetry—had said, 'The young woman has something in her.'"　This was strength to me coming from such a source.　Her own opinion of my few lines was, that they had more thought in them than many volumes of popular drawing room verse.　Still she advised me to write prose in preference.　Though I showed her letters to no one, the thought that I had such a noble, sympathizing friend, cheered my heart through many a dark hour.

From the year 1854 till her death, I had occasional kind letters from Mrs. Carlyle; in one

* See Appendix.

case, a very long one of four sheets, telling me for my encouragement of the hard-fisted life at Craigenputtock which she and her husband had to fight. A noble woman she was. When passing through Carlisle—perhaps, always when she stopped—she sent me word beforehand to meet her at the County Hotel.

Mrs. Carlyle was altogether an original little woman; natural and friendly to a degree, yet free from all littleness; free also from all provincial restraint of fashion or rank. She was very simply dressed in grey alpaca, most plainly made; not a frill, nor flounce, nor band anywhere about it; with a simple velvet skull cap, like a net over her brown hair; no brooch, or bracelet, or locket; but some very beautiful rings on one or two of her fingers. And her speech and manners were as simple as her person. No self-exhibition, which spoils almost all ladies; no prettiness, but grave, calm, natural truth and life.

In the presence of Mrs. Carlyle you felt that dress counted for nothing; the impression you made morally, spiritually, and intellectually being everything. Like a wise woman, she divined your tastes, and talked about what you wanted to hear, namely, the great Thomas and herself, but mostly of him. Of one thing she always made me feel certain, that I had made a good impression on her, and that she had neither pride nor distrust. She did not merely speak to you, but made you feel that she would like you to be entirely free and friendly with her. I found those whom I saw of this family singularly sincere. They talked to you as though they had known you all their lives.

Dr. John Carlyle came down to Finkle-street once to fetch me to see Mrs. Carlyle. It was July, and he was dressed in loose light clothing, very old fashioned in make, and a white hat. When I got to the County Hotel, I found him walking up and down in front, fearing, as he said, lest I should go to the wrong place. The second time I saw Mrs. Carlyle—when we were better acquainted—she kindly rose on my entering the room, and taking my hand, said with a definite Scotch accent: "Now come your ways, and sit ye down here by me (on the couch), and tell me how ye have been getting on."

The last time I saw her, after the first salutation —still holding my hand, and leading me to the couch on which she sat—she said kindly; "Come and sit ye down by me, and tell me all about yourself; what ye've been doing, and how ye're getting on." So she sat me down close beside her, and told me many things about herself and her home, and Thomas, as she invariably called him. Before leaving, she said: "I suppose you come to London sometimes. Everybody comes. Now, whenever ye do, be sure to come to Chelsea to see us."

Indeed, as Thomas Carlyle said in the last letter he wrote to me, when acknowledging a copy of the book I had dedicated to him: they had always regarded me as "one connected with their own household."

During her brief visits to the old border city of Carlisle, Mrs. Carlyle was very particular to keep herself from becoming known. On one occasion, she told me that Dr. Lonsdale* had pressed her very much to go to Rose hill, and see the garden; but she said they could not go (another lady being with her). The next time I met her, however, she was particularly careful to tell me the doctor had a con-

---

* Dr. Lonsdale, author of the "Worthies of Cumberland."
                                                            —*Ed.*

veyance waiting for them, and finding they had time to get back for the train, they went. In this, as in other matters, I saw she was anxious to leave a truthful impression of this small matter on my mind. She impressed me with her sincerity and kindly interest, telling me numberless simple incidents of her girlhood, among the rest that she once had an offer of marriage on the race course at Carlisle; all, as it seemed to me, to make me feel at home with her, and be free to speak without reserve in her presence.

No help, in the way I desired, came from my acquaintanceship with Mrs. Carlyle, and yet it was a help. I felt that I had been recognized as a fellow sufferer with higher and nobler souls than myself, and I felt encouraged and strengthened to hope and hold on my way. It is the fate of youth to see all things in roseate hues, and to believe most lives but their own happy. This was my tendency. Patience is our own strength. I had to learn the wisdom of waiting, which I gradually did. Our disappointments are the enduring metal of life, and harden us to still greater strength.

CHAPTER XX.

In all my sorrows, Work was my best helper; in
school and in my house. I was never quite free
from the old religious idea, that troubles were a
chastisement for moral delinquencies in heart or
life, sent to rouse and quicken forgetful men and
women, who had become indifferent, and had failed
to keep faithfully to the narrow path of religion.
This idea, ever real and living within me, always
prompted more moral carefulness; cutting off right
hands, and plucking out right eyes, sometimes, as
the case might be. The stern light of former vows
were revived within me, and I could often say of
a truth, "It is good for me to be afflicted."

So my sorrows were my strength. They opened
my eyes to the realities of life, and helped me to
shake myself free from the world's pretensions and
its mean complacencies. Because others did so,
why should I sell my soul for a mess of pottage?
So apart from churches and creeds, I learned the

divine strength of the soul, finding that its condemnation shamed me into higher thought and deed,
than any I could have got at church or chapel. In
fact, though I never did anything very grand, I
caught glimpses occasionally of that real life—the
light of the world—which stamps as paltry and
insignificant all its grandeurs, and elevates the
thoughts of man to that of the immortals.

The winter following the autumn, in which I had
the fever, was a very sad one to me. I opened my
school again, but people knew how very weak I
was, and so waited till I grew stronger before
sending their children. My girl, whom I had had
for five years, had given me notice to leave, before
my illness, and her time was up just as I returned
home, still very weak and unable to do anything
for myself. This tried me much. Mrs. Palmer,
seeing how weak I was, insisted that I should stay
with them for a week or so. I did so, but was very
anxious to go to my own home.

One evening, when no one was with me, I was
very unwell, and in great distress. Behold! the
door bell rang at that critical moment, and a young
person, the daughter of an old friend, had come to

see me and inquire how I was. After telling her all about myself, I said, "And now my great want is a nice girl to assist me. Do you know of one?" She sat a minute and then said, "Will you have me?" I replied, I should be delighted, but could not think of her giving up her business on my behalf.

Her father had left her two hundred pounds, and her mother being dead, she had established herself as a dressmaker. She still persisted, however, in coming, though I told her I could only give her eight pounds, the same as I had given the other girl. At last I said to her, "Well, go home and think over it for three days, and then come and tell me how you decide." This I insisted on; but she was back the next night, still in the same mind, very anxious to come.

So by God's special blessing and help, my trouble was ended—a very great one to me—and my need supplied. She stayed with me for twelve months, and proved herself more than I had expected. In that sad winter, when the doctors forbade me to read even, she made my long evenings cheery in my sorrow, by reading to me Maurice's Sermons, lent me by Dr. Lockie, and "Enoch Arden," by William Holstead.

The April after that, I think it was (for I am writing in great weakness), the Shakespeare Tercentenary was held. Carlisle, like other provincial towns, was in a puzzle what to do, or how to celebrate it. As a warm admirer of Shakespeare, I was anxious that something should be done. Sooner than that nothing should be done, I said to a gentleman, I would write an essay on the great Poet, a popular one on his character and the moral tendency of his works, in order to show to religious people generally the elevating and inspiring nature of his works.

From this, things soon flew into shape for a meeting, at which I was to give my essay. Through many hindrances, I got it worked out, but did not get it finished till the last day. The meeting, which was in the Athenæum, was a very large one. Mr. Robert Ferguson, M.P., was in the chair, and many of the clergy of the church and dissent were on the platform. My essay was well received, principally, I have no doubt, because I had made my remarks plain to the common understanding of the audience, and likewise I had made it my aim to interest them in Shakespeare, rather than to criticise him; and also to counteract the prevalent opinion in the religious world, that the study of his works was antagonistic to religion.

All my literary efforts were the results of some odd leisure moments. In this way I produced a small work, entitled "Old Castles." It was begun without much thought, as an account of a summer trip of Mr. Percival's Sunday school scholars, whom I accompanied to Corby Castle—this being the least careful of the lot; in fact, a mere newspaper sketch. I had often written cursory sketches of places I had visited, and they had been printed in various papers, such as the *Carlisle Observer.*

One fine Saturday afternoon in spring, Mrs. Fisher and I, and a little boy boarder, set off for Linstock Castle, only thinking of having a good walk and the benefit of breathing the fresh air. But the old castle, with its yard-wide walls, where kings and soldiers, and the famous Bishop Hilton, and monks, had alternately prayed and fought, with all the busy scenes of the dim past, inspired my imagination, and followed me—as things did then

—till I took the pen and put them on paper. So I wrote "Linstock Castle," a sketch.

I had no especial object in writing, and it laid aside for some time, till one day I saw an advertisement of the *Border Magazine*, to be published shortly in Edinburgh, and inviting contributions. I saw it would be the very place for my "Linstock Castle," though I knew it was very deficient as a history. It had been written merely as a rambling sketch of one of the many castles of Cumberland unknown to fame.

With hardly any improvement, I sent it to the editor, thinking it might be useful to him as material for his venture. In reply, he professed to be greatly obliged by my sending it, saying that it was written in popular readable style, which was very rare in such papers, "dry as dust" being the prevailing order. He pressed me to furnish him with further contributions, saying he hoped finally to be able to pay his contributors.

I replied that I was not able to leave my school to visit castles, but as I had never seen any popular sketch of Carlisle Castle, I would, if he liked, give a sketch of it. Accordingly, as was my wont, I began to do something in the way of jotting down ideas. I made it a complete study, seeking in every history I could get hold of for information on different points. The castle at that time being quite vacant of troops, I went in as often as I liked, often surprising the man in charge with facts of which he had no previous knowledge.

I got to like it much as I went on, and might have made much more of it if I had had time. Still I did not hurry, as the editor told me he would not have room for it till the following month. When completed, I let competent friends peruse and judge, a clergyman being among the number. All expressed themselves well pleased with it, one especially warned me strongly against trying to improve it, lest I should mar instead of mend. But after all the trouble I had taken with Carlisle Castle, it was destined not to appear in the *Border Magazine*.

The editor wrote that he was coming to Carlisle, and would call upon me, but this was not in my reckoning. Accordingly I wrote him a line, saying that I was a very busy woman, and would have no time to see him except on a Saturday, and scarcely then. But my fears of being troubled with the company of the editor were needless, for a report was soon in the wind that that gentleman had made a moonlight flitting; and with its second number the *Border Magazine* dropped into nonentity.*

I was too busy to think of literary matters, and it laid by for some time, till a young fellow, a Scotch student, came to Carlisle as editor of the *Express*. A friend introduced him to me as one who carried a copy of Bacon in his pocket. He stayed in Carlisle only a short time, but in that time he asked me to lend him the manuscript of "Carlisle Castle" to read privately. Without asking my leave, he printed part of it in the *Express*, and apologized for doing so by saying it would be largely read and appreciated. In this way was I obliged to consent that the remainder of it might appear. All my friends said, it was worthy of a far better place than the columns of a local newspaper.

A few months after, Lonsdale sent to say that some London publishers had written for leave to

* This is a mistake. The *Border Magazine* commenced in July, 1863, and was continued monthly until December of the same year. The article on "Linstock Castle" appeared in the November part.—*Ed.*

print it, and enquired what my will was respecting it. But I was offered nothing, so I declined. This induced me to see a local publisher, an intimate friend of mine, with a view of having my articles on "Old Castles" issued in a separate form. Linstock and Corby were mere sketches, and the poem on Carlisle was written as an after thought.

These were published in 1868, and made little impression in a collected form. Having been a good deal read before, they scarcely paid the expenses. And now after many years have passed, I have no regrets about this little book. Its composition as a literary labour—which was always a great joy to me—helped to inspire me with hope and courage in the lonely path of my woman's life, and to give a shade of additional dignity (always dear to me, as it should be to all women) to my character.

Before this period, I began to take an interest in the circumstances and conditions of woman's life. From the time I helped Mr. Wingrave with uneducated women and girls at the Damside, and the Messrs. Carr later, in their excellent schools for young women in Caldewgate—the helplessness of women in the great battle of life was enforced upon me, especially in large towns, where they are left so much to their own immature guidance, with often neither good habits nor influences nor education to help them. Consequently my attention was drawn to the Woman's Suffrage Society, formed by Miss Lydia Becker, and other ladies and gentlemen at Manchester. At once I saw that the inequality of the sexes in privilege and power, was a great cause of the dreadful hardships which women, especially in the lower classes, had to suffer.

The Quaker women, from George Fox's time, have been considered the equal and the peer of men, in all the councils of the church, in all the decisions of their meetings, and as missionaries and ministers, as well as in the home. In many ways, they have better ordered and more rational minds, better judgments, and more self control than others. They are not inflated with pride, but dignified with the native reason and the privilege of the use of equal gifts and capacities with men. I have come to the belief that in depriving women of their Rights, we have degraded them, and that England for that degradation suffers the curse of moral

I. 17

deterioration in her whole race. Great men, it is almost universally admitted, have always noble mothers.

We had an important meeting at Carlisle, at which Miss Becker was the principal speaker; and we afterwards formed a society, but our labours were not very successful in that direction. The practical northern mind will not make any pretence of believing what it does not believe, and has often little time for thought. I became warmly interested in all that concerns the interests of women. I worked and wrote whenever I could in favour of the Married Woman's Property Bill, and against that disgrace to humanity, the "C. D. Acts," which, thanks to the exertions of women, and Mr. Stansfield, are not what they were. I lectured on this subject to women to full audiences, and helped Mrs. Hudson Scott, who worked heartily in the cause, to get up petitions to Parliament against them. I feel great satisfaction, in looking back, that in the midst of a busy life, wherein my own head and hands had to supply every need, I tried to take a humble part in this cause, and still try to help with the helpers of women.

A life like mine had many disappointments; many a human reed on which I leaned broke, and I had many losses buried in my own bosom; for sorrow does but grow by talking about it. It was to my own heart I wrote most often, and out of my own heart I learnt in sorrow what I taught in song. My way was to open the sluice of some stirring rhyme, and let it flow off in song, which was like wine to my soul; and the test of its worth to me always was that the word, if inspired, gladdened me first; then I knew that it was likely to inspire and gladden others.

In this way I wrote "What to do," "Do thy Work," "Stand and Strive," and many others. These were all sent to the Carlisle newspapers— the *Journal* in the last years—and printed with my initials "M.S.," which I also used for letters and other papers. In writing on politics, which I often did, I used some other initial, "Z" very often, or other signature. I considered that if men knew who the writer was, they would say, "What does a woman know about politics?"

But the working men of Carlisle, I must say, made an exception in my favour, and more than once sought the help of my pen at election times. Through one election, a paper was published called "The Liberal Club," in which I did most of the writing. Under the assumed character of Mrs. Susan Trueman, the wife of John Trueman, the mother of a large family, I—as a woman who could hold the pen a bit—rattled away on behalf of my class against the Tories and taxation, when the younger children were asleep, and the eldest boy read the papers to me while rocking the cradle.

Also, as "Burns Redivivus," I parodied or adapted a lot of popular Scotch ballads, such as "There's nae luck aboot the house," "Scots wha hae," and "Auld lang syne." I likewise scribbled a lot of original doggerel which flew glibly on the popular tongue, and helped to turn the laugh on the Tories, if it did not bring conviction to them. I believe that was the election which Mr. W. Nicholson Hodgson lost, and Mr. Potter and Sir Wilfrid Lawson won. Dean Close, who had formerly voted "Blue," now joined the Tories, and I, under cover of some *outré* name, lectured him seriously about it.

Here's the tag end of one of the doggerel verses

which figured in the well read pages of the paper devoted to popular warfare, which if it did nothing else helped to keep up the fun.

> So give the Dean a surplice clean,
>   And W. N. his stick ;
> He'll have to walk, and soon, I ween,
>   So let him have it quick.

I also wrote on many other topics; the practical well-being of the middle and working classes being my aim. Various were the themes I took up besides politics. Drink, especially, I wrote much against, seeing much in my walks of the poverty it inflicted, in the blue-white faces and rags of the many poor little shivering children I met. Many and many a time had I to pull my veil down, and speed on with bowed head, to hide a face streaming with sorrow for those poor little innocents, which often led me to write strongly in their behalf, when I got home.

I wrote earnestly in behalf of coffee shops, helping to demolish the many fallacies brought against them, nor ceased until they were fairly well established in the city. A great convenience these places have been everywhere, and I have no doubt a means of

much good; for there the country boy and girl, and
the tired man and woman, can refresh themselves
for a penny, nor fear acquiring habits of evil or
intemperance. I could not take part on committees,
nor help in the practical work of furthering the
scheme. The one thing I could do I did, and that
was to try to inspire others with the importance and
useful nature of the work.

It would indeed demand more time than I have
at command, to describe half of what I wrote about
"Woman's Suffrage," "Marriage with a Deceased
Wife's Sister," and the "Employment of Women."
But I was always pleased that I had essayed to
write two or three letters, which had been the
means of helping two worthy families, and one
very worthy woman.

The first in point of time was the case of old Mr.
Morrison of Cummersdale. I had known him for
some years, through having his daughter, a pupil
teacher, lodging at my house. Though a learned
man in mathematics, the classics, and some of the
modern languages, he had been obliged to give up
a good school, and undertake the humbler duties
of a village one, through being almost drawn double

by rheumatism. About ten o'clock one dark wintry night—after teaching a French class at the Mechanics' Institute, in Fisher-street—in plodding his way homeward, with his head bowed down, as was his wont, on coming to the side of the river Caldew, it is supposed, he missed his foothold, fell in, and was drowned.

He was a man I had admired, as despite of all difficulties, he was always engaged with private or public tuition, keeping his family respectable, and placing them out in the world at his own expense. Such men as these, I always thought most worthy of honour. And seeing his family so suddenly deprived of every means of support, I at once wrote to the *Journal* a strong letter, urging his family's claims, in their forlorn condition, to some subscription in their behalf.

My letter had been well timed. Money came in apace. The subscription list mounted up and grew to sixty-five or seventy pounds, which must have been a great help to the poor widow and her family. I was exceedingly pleased, but never named myself in conjunction with it ; my joy being that the thing should prosper, and the family should derive benefit from it.

Another of these cases occurred, I think, a year or two after. It was that of Mr. Thomas Hardy of Caldewgate. He worked at Dixon's factory, and had done so from his youth. The first time I saw him was at Mr. Osborn's night school, when Mr. Osborn taught grammar, logic, etc., to working men. Afterwards he became a very earnest and enthusiastic politician, lecturing and speaking continually for the Liberal party, to which he was a considerable help.

For several years he was one of the leading men among his own party—a man who had largely cultivated his own mind, and was especially well read in history and politics. He was also a careful, steady, religious man, and had a nice cottage house of his own. Consumptive for long before he died, he left his wife and large family entirely without provision, save this house, which he was most anxious should not be sold, but remain for the use of the family. At his death, I thought that the family of a man who had so largely devoted his time and talents to the success of the Liberal cause in Carlisle, and who had always conducted himself in an exemplary way, ought to have something done for them.

Accordingly I took the first opportunity to send to the newspaper a sketch of his life, appealing to a generous public to do something out of respect to his memory, for the education of his younger children and the assistance of his household. This was very kindly responded to, and the subscriptions mounted to a considerable sum. Mr. Potter and Sir Wilfrid Lawson, the members for Carlisle, sent twenty pounds each, which with other sums raised it to over eighty pounds. This proved a great help to Mrs. Hardy in her time of need; she was a woman in every respect worthy of her exemplary husband. Their little home was a model of domestic neatness, and its books, maps, and pictures, proved it to be one of intelligence and peace.

The next case, which occurred a year or more after, but unlike it in kind, was that of my friend Mrs. Fisher, well known and kindly remembered by the people of Carlisle. From an early period I had been acquainted with Mrs. Fisher, having been introduced to her by another literary friend, Mr. James Walker. As her house was not far from mine, I often ran to see her for a bit of congenial talk; but I soon found that she, like most women of mind, lived a life of trouble. She had a husband, it is true, but he thought more of the money value of her gifts than of anything else, and would call her up early on a winter morning to finish a tale for the few pounds to be got by it.

A small talker and an opium eater, he was the glibbest and most courteous while indulging in public houses. Often have I met the poor wife speechless and tearful, on a Saturday night, posting off to get him something for his supper. He was a carpenter by trade, working on his own account, and had an apprentice, a poor sickly fellow, who had no home but with them.

They had no children, and had it not been for the wife's exertions, their comforts would have been few and far between. When I first knew her, she had a wide repute as a writer of local poetry, and had published a volume or two. These she took about with her to sell, and generally met with success. She had then begun to write tales, for which she found a ready market, either in the local papers, or in several instances in Cassell's publications, though she only got about five pounds each for them. For one whose education was limited, she had a mind of no ordinary capacity, being shrewd, well read, and intelligent. As it was, she stood alone among the women of Carlisle in the dexterous use of her pen. By her husband's death, she was left with greater freedom to do as she liked.

Before this, however, she had set up as a public letter writter, and afterwards she opened a school for working men's children. With these she fought on very comfortably till her health failed, and then every one saw she had not strength for her labour. At last she was obliged to give up, but was without any certain means of support. Previous to this, however, Mr. Hardy had got up a subscription, which had helped her considerably. But now with failing health, and her means all gone, though she said nothing, it was evident she was very sad.

Calling one night to see how she was, her sadness and changed appearance moved me deeply, and as I went home I resolved to write something there and then on her behalf. I wrote a short but very stirring appeal in favour of a fund being raised, which should be continued to her weekly, so that she might feel sure of a small sufficiency. I suggested my friend, Miss Palmer, as one who, I felt sure, would be willing to receive any money entrusted to her, and would see it dispensed regularly for Mrs. Fisher's comfort.

The next morning—thanks to the editor of the *Journal*—my joy was great. I saw my letter in the paper; and before the close of the same day, I had the satisfaction of knowing that its mission had been happily fulfilled, and that many kind and generous citizens had responded to my appeal. It is not now in my power to name any, with the exception of Robert Ferguson, Esq., M.P., who headed the subscription list with half-a-crown per week from that time forward.

Dear always to me in after life, was the recollection of the prompt action of my letter, and its effect upon the good people of the Border city; especially when I went to Mrs. Fisher's home and saw her kept clean and comfortable, and free from her old cares and worry. Women with a tendency to learning or literature in the lower ranks, in times past, had to work hard for very little recompense. Mrs. Fisher had a troubled life, but like a prudent and proud woman, as she was, she kept these things to herself. Poverty was the goad that led her to write tales, read publicly, and do many other of the best things she did.

I may say that among my many enterprises to do a little good in a lowly way, to my own sex, I soon after this time gave six lectures to women, on Sunday evenings, in the Temperance Hall, Caldewgate. My object was to gain over some of the many slovenly women, who stand hour after hour at their door posts, satisfying their inane spirits, by watching the ever varying incidents of the streets. I spent only half-a-crown on a few handbills to make it known, and this was all it cost me, independent of the intellectual exertion I bestowed on it.

As to the lectures themselves, I aimed to speak in a plain, practical, and colloquial manner on practical matters, not exclusively religious—or such as are so called—on the training of children both physical and moral; on the duty and advantages of thrift, cleanliness, good manners, purity of spirit, cheerfulness, and goodwill; together with many other things conducive to the peace and prosperity of families, not often touched on in sermons, nor thought, by many, altogether fit subjects for Sundays, though, I think, they might be with profit.

No great number came to hear me, but those who did were poor women, though not all of the class intended. One of the things I insisted on was the worth of trifles, and the spirit in which things are done. I cannot remember at this length of time, the subjects of all my lectures. One only has vividly remained with me, and, I think, I enjoyed the delivery of it more than any other, though they were all much alike. I called it "Making and Mending;" and first of all I led my small audience up to the great Maker and Mender, and made them see, with David, the Heaven as the *work* of His fingers, and how from everlasting to everlasting they repeat His praise.

I always felt deeply when describing nature. In asking them to think simply of the morning made gloriously anew out of every dark night, it was an easy task to lead them to listen. I endeavoured also to depict how simple women could beautify their small homes, and make them, as I had seen sometimes, when some blind was undrawn, or some door left ajar, snug and comfortable with pictures, and genteel comforts that cost little.

So also I told them by attention they might *mend* their little ones' manners, and lead them to practice it as a diversion, while they were sewing, or even washing. I told them that the good housewife is as holily employed when she sits by her neat hearth and makes "auld claithes look amaist as weel as new," for her boys' and husband's comfort, as if she were at the prayer meeting. I ended by saying, that the very spirit of such a mother, filled with the idea of her family's moral good, comfort, and happiness, could not fail to elevate and bless them, and be the means of bettering their fortunes in this world, and leading them to thoughts and hopes of the blessedness of the world beyond. This is a simple outline of one of my little lectures to plain women.

But, oh! what an outcry was raised against me by the religious world! All parties agreed with each other in denouncing my little effort to interest and enlighten women. "To think," they said, "of my beginning an address on a Sunday night without singing and prayer! Such a thing was awful and unheard of." My girl, who was much attached to me, every time she went out came back with such a sad face, saying mostly, "O Miss Smith, what things folk do say about you. It's no use my replying that it's very good what you say. They won't believe me." But I troubled nothing. The working men urged me to keep on, believing it would do good. They offered me the hall, with gas and fire, free. The women also urged me to continue my addresses.

CHAPTER XXI.

In going along the Castle-bank for an evening stroll, over the bridge towards Rickerby, quite unlike other ladies, it may be, whose sole attention was engrossed by dress and fashion, I saw nothing but the sorrows and evils around me. Often and often I was told by kind friends, that they had met me, but that I had never seen them; while others came laughingly up to me, to recall me from my thoughts by the reality of their presence.

At that time the Sauceries were held of the Corporation by a well-to-do citizen, and nightly, all through summer time, his man, "the shepherd," patrolled the field with an awful looking cudgel in his hand, to the great alarm and terror of little boys and girls, who fled with their little naked feet helter-skelter before him; the smaller ones often falling in their flight and sometimes hurting themselves badly, when much crying ensued.

The "bobby," too, was a terrible scare. His

helmet was the signal for the same rush and precipitate flight of old and young, the very little ones crying bitterly in their ineffectual efforts to get away, being often left by their bigger companions.

One night, having been detained at home, I was flying with some speed over the grass down to the side of the Caldew—one of my favourite walks in hot weather, which I always thought should be laid to that river for a park—when this veritable shepherd, with his staff, chanced to spy me. He shouted and held it up ominously, but was, I fancy, rather taken aback when he saw me alter my course, and trip over the grass to meet him. He put down his staff and stood still, however, and then I in my turn catechised him, as to whether his master did not take the ground—as I had been told by members of the Corporation—subject to the condition of its being run over by children and others.

This, and other encounters between the police and small boys (who roar aloud for fear of being taken up by the men in blue,) I sent to the papers, shocked to see English children so persecuted for indulging in their divinest instinct—the love of nature—and gathering a few wild flowers. And my letters were much read, my initials "M.S." being well known. I wrote to convince, and often had the conviction that they had weight in the proper quarters, and not unfrequently produced the desired effect. Thus the children were less persecuted after this, and were not disturbed when gathering flowers or chasing butterflies; while the elder boys wrestled in north country fashion, or played their sturdier games, if not to their hearts' content, certainly more freely and with more enjoyment.

Indeed, I found much to write about in my walks. I wrote pleading for seats behind the castle and along the banks of the Eden, long before any were put down, as an inducement for the aged especially to get out into the open air. Very pleased was I, when I saw workmen accomplishing one more good thing mostly in behalf of the working classes, and those two ends of humanity so often forgotten—old men and little children.

I wrote also about the levelling of the Sauceries long before it was done, seeing how much an "observing eye" could find to beautify the outskirts of the city, for the delight of its toiling thousands, and the joy of the passing stranger. Very much was I surprised again to see this being commenced with two or three years after, heedless of what I had done, but glad of the idea becoming a reality.

As a last and most effective example of my letter writing, and the results it produced, I give this instance, which occurred nearly twenty years ago, perhaps more. The Castle-bank lies close under the castle, and at the back of Finkle-street, where I lived and had my school for twenty-four years. Leading down by the Eden from it, is a beautiful walk known as the "Weavers'-bank," so called from having been made by unemployed weavers in times of depression. It is one of the most beautiful, healthy, and most frequented walks in the city, and has always been so.

But at the time when this occurred, just after the French invasion scare, Carlisle castle was, and had been for two years or more, quite full of soldiers. Over these men no very strict discipline seemed to have been exerted. In the evenings of all days alike, they overflowed into Finkle-street, and on the bank, stopping up the gates, where they especially congregated. They made riot and used profusely disreputable language, with disreputable girls, big and little, who met them there every evening for the purpose of this coarse obscene mirth. The noise and sight were disgusting to every passer by, but especially so to ladies and mothers with girls by their sides.

One Sunday in early summer, a bright and beautiful evening, I left my house for a long walk up the Brampton-road. The gates leading to the Castle-bank were crowded with a noisy, obstreperous, coarse multitude, as was the path between them, ladies and gentlemen being hardly able to pass. I heard a gentleman behind me say to a lady, who accompanied him, "What a place this is! And on a Sunday night! And no police!" No, never a policeman to be seen, though they were always on the track of the poor little children gathering a few flowers in the fields.

With some difficulty I got through, and sped on towards Stanwix-bank, where I met a lady with her girls, whom I knew. We had not stood long, till she said, "Oh! Miss Smith, what a place that bank has become! I used to go round there for a walk in the evening, but I daren't do so now,

Those soldiers and rough girls behave so shamefully, and use such disgusting language. I wish you would write about it to the paper." I said I was afraid, they were such a rough lot; and anything I could do I feared would be ineffectual.

So we parted, but I could not help thinking about it. It followed me, as such things sometimes did, and on the Monday evening I sat down to write a letter to the *Journal* on the subject. I neither took much time nor pains. My letters were always the strong sense and feeling which the first thoughts on the subject evolved. If the matter flowed freely and kept my pen busy, I kept on; if not, I put it aside—which rarely happened—as a thing not to spend time upon. That night my pen flew fast. I was on a familiar theme—how standing armies demoralize the community; one of their worst evils, perhaps; and my mind was full of the subject.

Living in Finkle-street so long, close to the castle, I had seen much of soldiers and had endured much, both by night and day, from their loud and lawless mirth and bickerings. So my letter—not a very long one, but full of indignant fire—was finished and sent up to the *Journal* the same night. The only precaution I took, was that I did not sign any name likely to lead to my identification. The next morning I saw it in the paper, but thought nothing more about it till the evening, when I started for my usual walk between six and seven.

When I got to the bank gates, which were quite quiet, I saw a group of angry-looking, white-aproned, bonnetless girls, standing in the distance, straining their eyes towards the gate, evidently expecting their usual compeers. I entered the gate and walked on a short distance, when a big boy seeing them, shouted out, "Hey! ye needn't wait. It's been i' the papers, an' they're nut comin' to-neet." The girls were confounded, but made off round the castle, to see for themselves.

This made me feel somewhat nervous, for I saw it was my doing. But on looking up, as I went on, what was my alarm to see a double file of soldiers marching towards me, with officers behind them, and in the distance a policeman hurrying on. What I felt at that moment, it would be vain to attempt to describe. My limbs seemed powerless to support me, and I trembled so that I could not get on. I thought all eyes were fixed on me, policeman's and all, and that they would know me to be the woman. I tried to look another way, but thought this would betray me, and assumed a face of indifference I could not well sustain.

So they passed me, but I trembled for long after; and as soon as I reached home again, I hurried off to Mrs. Fisher, and made her my confidante of the whole thing, for I dare tell no one else. She was frightened, too, at the part I had essayed. "Hinny," said she, "you must be careful, or they will break your windows, and serve you out in a shameful manner. Don't tell another creature." And then she told me for my comfort her own escapades in writing in political catches and squibs; and how she had once to run up a lane to hide herself, and remain a prisoner there for nearly an hour.

Next day and the next day after again, I heard of the soldiers—lately so great a pest to the bank— being under discipline everywhere; officers marching behind them with naked swords, all over the astonished city; and the bank and Finkle-street were once more passable and quiet, Sundays and week days. Now that the soldiers had been cleared off, the girls no longer came. Previously their behaviour had been enough to corrupt any little girl that went by. Some officer wrote to the paper rebuking the writer of the letter for making the thing so public.

I thought I was unknown, till a few days after, walking on the bank, I met some lady friends, who began to compliment me on the great good my letter had done, saying how glad people were that the thing had been taken in hand. For once, I dare not own my handiwork; so I said there were other ladies who could write a good letter, and they must not be too sure of its being mine. I had to exercise caution, as I soon found I had a rough element around me ready to take vengeance whenever an opportunity occurred.

One Saturday afternoon, I happened to be leaving my door, when some factory lasses were passing. They all stopped, turned back, and stared. One of them pointed fiercely to me, and hissed out, "That's hur! I tell ye, that's hur!" Though I tried hard to look haughty, and walked away, it made me tremble sadly, as I did not know what might come next. Thank heaven, I got nothing worse! But

I felt gratified (as I always did when my letters effected any good) when I saw what a change was wrought for the better by it, in all the neighbourhood.

From that time, the soldiers were never allowed to congregate on the bank, nor in Finkle-street. It was such a complete change that everybody took notice of it, and talked about it. Going to the door, two or three years after this event, to see the cause of an unusual noise, I found my neighbour there also, and in reply to my question, she said: "It's them soldiers again. They'll git in the paper as they did afore, if they don't mind." This pleased me well, as I saw she knew nothing of its being my doing, so I replied: "And quite right it should be so."

But this stir caused by my letter occurred just before midsummer, my usual time for spending a month in Oxfordshire, at my native village of Cropredy, famous for its "fight" between Waller and King Charles I. of blessed memory; and far away among its rich grass and cornfields and sweet blossomy roadsides—and here my terror of the retaliation of the soldiers all disappeared.

CHAPTER XXII.

IT was soon after this occurrence I published a second volume of poetry, which I called "Progress and other Poems." I had for a long time been engaged in composing the longest piece—that is, "Progress," having begun it in 1865. It was rather a rash undertaking for one with so little time on hand as I had. But like many a nobler and truer poem, it was written as a solace for a great and undivulged sorrow. This trouble was augmented by the loss of a minister of religion, whose services I had attended nearly all the time he was in Carlisle. This was the Rev. W. R. Percival, a true christian gentleman, and a man of advanced views, with which views I truly sympathized, as did many others in the old city.*

But when Mr. Percival and his family were gone, I felt their loss very much, from our close intimacy; and having a sad heart sorrow as well, I turned for

* See account of Mr. Percival, page 231.

solace and support to poetry, contemplating some larger and more ambitious effort solely as a cure for my melancholy mind. Hence the origin of "Progress," which in some measure came from my reading Emerson, together with my study of history, and also from my admiration of the poetry of Ebenezer Elliot, the strong spirited corn-law rhymer. Of Elliot's heart-stirring verse there is, I think, some forgetfulness in England in our flippant times; but whose strong rugged lyrics the Americans still highly value and preserve.

Pondering this enterprise, one Sunday afternoon as I walked to Brunstock bridge, in the fair harvest time, I composed the first stanza of it, not doing anything more for months. But the strength, effect, and sweetness of Elliot's poetry, who was an unlearned man, greatly encouraged me; and in the sad winter which followed, I made some way with the first part of it, as I found it the best solace for my trouble.

I told no one of my design. I expected nothing but failure for a long time; distrust of my own powers being one of the chief demons I had to conquer. But poetry, as Coleridge says, is its own exceeding reward, and so I found it. It not only healed my heart, but it elevated my mind, raising it not only above sorrow, but above sin, and keeping me true to the great thoughts and inspirations which it produced.

Much of it was produced while at household work, which required my hands only, leaving my head free to work out my ideas and to form them into verse. I had many troubles and slights to endure, and sometimes much scorn; but the joy of my poetry effaced them all, and truly "none of these things moved me" while that prospered, which was not always the case.

I could do little or nothing at my poetry, save on a Sunday, when it was the sweetener and uplifter of my day. It helped to make me happy, though I was devoid of the joys of family and friends. After Mr. Percival left, I could find no Nonconformist church with which I could ally myself. Brought up with all the strong prejudices and predilections of dissent, I had a very great objection to the formalities of the church. The very singing in the church seemed theatrical to me, and appeared to crush out the spirituality of everything it sings,

I once heard Newman's "Lead kindly light,"
which had long been a great delight and inspiration
to me, sung in Carlisle Cathedral—when I went to
hear the Rev. John Oakley preach, then its new
dean—and the singing shocked me. All its fine
spirituality was gone, and from that time I had to
forget what I had heard in the cathedral, before I
could again enjoy that holy hymn—a soul's cry,
indeed. I have always believed with Emerson that
it is the soul that sings. It was that which made
Sankey's singing so divine.

Alone in my secret meetings with God, I found
great strength on my knees, face to face with Him
who seeth in secret. I knew an old friend, who
used to kneel before God, after all were gone to
bed, till midnight, often till her voice was lifted in
a soft song of praise.

Singularly enough, I could never forget any verse
that was good. It would cleave to my memory till
I took it up again and adopted it. A friend once
asked me what was the cause of the great strength
he always found in my poetry. "Shall I tell you?"
I said, "I never compose till after much prayer,
nor until the spirit mounts freely." Of course,

there were exceptions to this rule, but they were rare with me.

In composing " Progress," I read much and studied much in various histories, and devoted much patient thought to many points unthought of by the casual reader. Its proper title, indeed, ought to have been, "Religion: the Source and Soul of all true Religion," for it was really a Religious poem, and was meant to be taken as such.

Two readers only, so far as I know, recognized it in this light. These two read themselves into its life and spirit. One was my old and honoured friend, Mr. William Sutton of Scotby, who always kindly appreciated any effort of mine. He read it through to his family, night by night, marked what he admired, and, not waiting till I could go over, wrote me a long letter to tell me how he admired both its spirit and tone; saying, in conclusion, that he hoped it might be a blessing to many, as he was sure it ought to be.

The other was a Scotch scripture reader, who had borrowed the book from a friend. He had read it as religious Scotchmen usually do read

books—thoroughly and with great gusto.   He also
wrote me a letter, expressing his great admiration
of its religious spirit, together with many fervent
expressions about its influence, and the good such a
book must do.

Singular, not one of its reviewers noticed this, or
even seemed to suspect it.   One said it was very
true to the history of England, but said nothing
about its being true to Religious history.   An
Oxford paper, in a few words, perhaps did me the
most justice.   It pointed out that my poetry was
characterized by deep thought, and though perhaps
not to be classed in the first rank, was yet worthy
of an honourable place.   Others showed me, by
what they said of it, that they had never looked
into it, or could not distinguish between faithful
labour and poetical trifling.

Mrs. Carlyle's judgment of my first venture,
"that there was more thought in it, than in many
volumes of drawing room poetry," was quite true
of the next attempt.   Like all second rate poets, I
lacked imagination, and believed too much in the
lower powers of will and continuous study.   Some
few of the minor poems attained a more poetic

height.   One or two of them, by others more than by myself, were thought excellent.   Latterly, I was pleased to know they were read by working men, in reading rooms, news rooms, etc.

Mr. Sutton of Scotby took a large number of my books, as did Mr. Robert Ferguson of Morton, M.P., and one or two other friends.   The *Carlisle Journal* and the *Carlisle Patriot* reviewed it very fairly ; the latter saying, "It was noble in every line ;" and the former, that, "Like Tennyson, I knew the secret of going round and round a subject, till I had extracted all its substance."   The *Banbury Guardian*, one of my native county papers, also reviewed it well, noting especially my truthfulness of description, in a very appreciative manner.

My school was now at its best.   I had from time to time raised my terms, yet still had plenty of applications.   I had a great many country girls, nearly grown up, the daughters of farmers, who wanted to have a little finish in a town school.   For the last ten or fifteen years or more, nearly half of my pupils were women grown.   I could also have had ladies as private pupils.   I had now got to be known as a woman of some learning; and if my last volume of poetry had brought me no money, it had increased my fame for knowledge.

The people of Cumberland understood and appreciated me; and I in return, admired their thrift, love of work, independence, and hardihood —the country people being nearly all of this type.

CHAPTER XXIII.

As I got a little means gathered together, I began to have a feeling that I should help any one I could belonging to my own family. I had therefore taken my eldest brother's daughter to live with me, with the intention of training her to be a governess. My brother—a man of intellectual tastes and tendencies—had little liking for business, and consequently had not succeeded in it.

I thought to train their daughter to get her own living, thinking that perhaps she might also be able to do something to help her parents. But in a few months the poor thing, a girl of seventeen, never very strong, began to droop. At the beginning of winter she caught cold, and altered suddenly for the worse during the night. On the following morning, in an hour or two after coming down stairs, she died, having on her travelling dress, and all things ready for starting for home.

Thus alone in the world, I stood almost stunned,

with my dead niece in the silent chamber. I felt a mother's grief, yet with the necessity of one who had to see to the ordering of all things solely herself. My brother arrived early the next morning. Almost his first words were, "I am glad she has died here, as I don't think she would have lived long. And, oh! such work we had to get poor James buried!"

This event occurred before the Act was passed which enabled dissenters to have their own minister to bury their dead. My brother's son, a youth of nineteen, who died unbaptised, had been the cause of much trouble to his parents in his burial. During the poor boy's illness of gastric fever, the clergyman had gone several times to his parents' house, worrying them to let him borrow a large brewing tub at the "Lion" public house, in which to baptize him before his death, ill as he was!

In vain they told him their son had been converted and baptised with the Holy Spirit, and that it was not required. He persisted in urging that unless the youth were baptised he could not have christian burial. At last he was told plainly, they could not consent to such a course, and then— he shook the dust from off his feet and departed!

Poor James died and was buried in the village churchyard, without bell or book or priest, amid a group of shuddering village onlookers, full of sympathy for the lad; and his parents, full of condemnation of priests and their intolerance and vindictive rule. Would that the Church of England could see itself as others see it; even as the illiterate village dissenter sees it! Verily, it would lead to truer ideas of right and justice.

We buried the poor girl decently in the cemetery at Carlisle, a Wesleyan minister conducting a short but feeling service. I did what I could to lighten my brother's grief, and paid all expenses. But what a sad winter ensued for me! Through all the dark months, that pale young face was ever before me, and my evenings became so sad that I was often driven to walk forth into the streets, to dissipate the pressing sadness that would cleave to me, in spite of every effort to shake it off.

From the first I had been careful of my means, and had always thought it right to save something out of whatever my income might be. Mr. David Blackburn, of the Carlisle and Cumberland Bank, an old friend of mine, kindly offered to invest anything I might have to spare. I wished him to invest it in Carlisle and Cumberland Bank shares. But after waiting some time, he sent me a note, saying he had been offered ten shares in the City and District Bank. Would I take these? I accepted them, and afterwards added others, and found they paid very well for a long time. I had a few likewise in the Carlisle and Cumberland Bank, as time went on, and I could spare the means. But I held the proceeds of my money to be sacred; not to be spent, but carefully reserved for the future, when I might not be able to work.

As for fine raiment, or jewellery, or fine furniture, I had no ambition that way. A lover of learning and literature can dispense with these things. Needful and comfortable things, and things be-fitting one's position, avoiding all singularity of manner or appearance, I made an aim of having. All else I thought it right to do without; nor was I ever ashamed of being plainly dressed.

Indeed, I used to say I could do without dress, as I found I got more respect with my plain dress, than others did with much finery. The truth is, I never could bear myself in new clothes, or in anything like finery. Dress was rarely in my thoughts, unless I chanced to be told by some female friend that I was really getting very shabby, and then I had to bestir myself. As for fashion, I was always old fashioned.

I had my dresses made as a matter of economy. I also thought to have them of good material; often saying, that I could not afford cheap things. What other women delighted in, I hated, and had done so from a girl—namely, shopping. I always put it off as long as I could, and at last I went simply because I was obliged to go.

But to return to my shares. They did very well until the City of Glasgow Bank broke, precipitating so many people of limited means into indigence. This event created a feeling of insecurity in the country, which acted injuriously on many provincial banks, and aroused the fears of trustful country people. My bank—the City and District—was obliged to make certain changes in order to meet the emergency, and as a natural consequence, the shares fell greatly.

It was a trying year to me, who had no resource but my own earnings. All I had saved was invested in these bank shares. Along with others, I felt it acutely, fearing the worst, as people usually do. However, the constant advice of Mr. Blackburn was of great use to me. It kept me more patient, perhaps, than I otherwise should have been. He helped me to understand the whole course of action and probable result; and assured me that finally things would all come right—which eventually came true.

My losses were great for one like me, who had known the tug of war; and they finally proved to be something like £300. At first, this greatly affected my mind, and darkened my existence with a night which nothing but prayer could lift. But in proportion to the depth of darkness caused by my trouble—overwhelming at first—was the buoyancy of my mind in finally rising above it. Thus after a brief interval of intense sadness, I thought no more of it, than though it had never been; and I was soon able to resume my old occupations of thought and poetry as steps upward into the sunshine again.

After attending assiduously for a month or more, the sick bed of one of my nephews, who was staying with me in Carlisle, I had the misfortune to be cast down by a serious illness, which proved to be a complication of typhoid fever and inflammation of the lungs. As I was in a very critical condition—it was, indeed, a struggle between life and death—I had to have two medical men, Dr. Elliot and Dr. Lockie.

My great misery was that I could get no rest. I never slept for five nights. I was haunted by strange unearthly sights, which continually flitted before my mental vision, and though I knew them to be only the illusion of the brain and the outcome of my disease, I prayed most earnestly that I might not lose my reason.

At this critical period, Mr. and Mrs. Palmer, who then lived in Abbey-street, stood by me as sympathizing friends. Their eldest daughter, formerly a pupil of mine, had just finished her education in Edinburgh. She very kindly offered to take what remnant of my school was left, and bring them forward to the best of her ability. This I most gratefully accepted. I felt their kindness in an inexpressible degree—a kindness I never could nor ever can repay.

My loss by this illness was very great, as I had no resource to fall back upon but the savings of my own economy. As soon as I was a little better, the first thing I did was to send my girl up street to pay the few small bills that had accumulated. To my surprise, she came back with the money in her hand, saying, all alike had refused to take anything. "Not till Miss Smith is quite well again, and able to come herself," they said, "will we take the money." This and other acts of simple personal kindness and sympathy overpowered me with feelings of gratitude to these trustful friends and others.

END OF AUTOBIOGRAPHY.

CHAPTER XXIV.

IT now only remains for the editor to supply a few brief notes in conclusion.

Miss Smith—as she has stated—toiled and struggled through many years to become possessed of a moderate competency for old age. She denied herself all luxuries and non-essentials, and lived the life of a Spartan. Her food was plain; her furniture was plain; and her dress—according to the standard of the girl of the period—was plainer still. Indeed, it may be said that not unfrequently her dress was decidedly antiquated and old fashioned.

As she approached the age of sixty, her health became precarious and changeable; and after a few years it fairly broke down, which necessitated her relinquishing her school duties altogether. Like many another poor mortal, the time of unclouded old age and rest from labour (about which she had fondly dreamed) never came. Thus her favourite country walks became more and more circumscribed, and at last had to be finally given up.

Her affections clung so closely around the old house in Finkle-street, and the plot of ground behind, that she could scarcely separate herself from them. In one of her letters she says: " The usual term of my house expires at Whitsuntide. Though I have no one belonging to me in Carlisle, my heart grows sad at the thought of finally leaving the old place."

She was induced to try the more salubrious climate of southern England, and she took up her abode for a short time with one of her nephews, at Richmond, on the Thames, and from thence she removed to Twickenham.

After a time, however, life became irksome to her in the south. She sighed to be back within sight of the blue hills of the "North countrie," and wrote touching and pathetic appeals to that effect to her friends in Cumberland. It soon became evident that there was no rest for the sole of her foot but at Carlisle, and not for any length of time even there. With shattered nerves and great difficulty in breathing, she returned again to the old Border city. It was quite evident to her old acquaintances, that her malady was gaining upon her. At times life dragged on so wearily and monotonously—with scarcely a perceptible ebb or flow—that her fervent prayer was, to be released from her sufferings.

A friend, on calling upon her about this period, found her in a state of much consternation. "Oh, dear! oh, dear! What think you?" she exclaimed. "Mrs. —— (in the next room there) sat sulking the whole of last Sunday afternoon, with an open Bible on her knee, never speaking a single word to poor me, and seemingly quite oblivious to any of my simple wants. Do you call *that* Christianity? I call it worse than heathenism!"

Miss Smith has drawn a very truthful and painstaking picture of herself, with its varied lights and shades of character, in the foregoing Autobiography. The story which she tells of her connection with the Osborn family, is one of almost incredible nature; and yet, can anyone doubt its veracity? No person of any penetration at all, I think, can fail to see that truth is stamped on every page. Her unceasing craving for intellectual intercourse, and her intense love for the higher class of literature, no doubt, had something to do with it. But much deeper than those was her warm human sympathy, set into action by the manifold sufferings of an unfortunate and friendless family.

She was one of the most truthful spoken of Adam's race it has been my fortune to know, with any kind of intimacy. In cases where she did overshoot the mark, the delusion was part and parcel of her own nature. She had become unconsciously to believe what she spoke or set forth.

Your clever or intellectual woman is invariably a woman with a will of her own, and Miss Smith was no exception to this rule; and she certainly could be stately when occasion required.

Miss Smith may be taken as a fair specimen of a class of clever amateur authors, ever buoyant and full of hope that the coy jade Fame will not give them the go-by altogether; a class of authors considerable in all ages, but never more numerous than at present. And what an unprofitable game the publication of most books is to the great majority of outside authors who write them! Miss Smith has told the tale of the slow dragging sale, and of the no sale at all, which followed the issuing of the two volumes of poetry put forth at different periods of her life. One of her scholars often related, in a jocular manner, how he made kite tails out of her poems, when attending her school, and, by this means, caused the genius in them to take higher flight than ever it had done before !

Miss Smith held no exaggerated opinion of her own abilities. Her ambition did not soar into the clouds. She says very laudably and sensibly : " I hope in some of my verses—in a few pictures from nature, at least—I may finally stand with Miss Blamire."

She is seen at her best in her poems founded on Home and the Social Affections. "The Snow Storm" was suggested to her while returning home one Sunday afternoon in winter, from the cemetery at Carlisle, when the snow lay thick on the ground, and the sun was going down, round and red, in the western sky, and the distant objects were partially obscured by a thin film of white mist. This piece has always appeared to me to be the most masterly one she produced. It contains much deft and delicate work, closely studied from nature. How truthfully depicted, for example, are the fears and ultimate despair which crush the mother's heart !

Another very perfect and finely conceived piece,

is the one entitled "February," This short poem
is almost as fruitful in thought and suggestion as
one of Jean Paul's Fruit, Flower, and Thorn pieces.
It contains verses not unworthy of the old drama-
tists of Queen Elizabeth's time, which might have
received the commendation of Charles Lamb.
Take, for instance, the following :—

> With nature sweet he bears it high,
> 　A braggart, threat'ning face he wears ;
> If he must die his corpse shall lie
> 　In warrior state, he loud declares.
>
> He'll have no garlands round his head,
> 　No foolish trappings of young flowers ;
> But better fitting these instead—
> 　The missiles keen of his own hours :
>
> Snow, hail, and rain, shall mark where lies
> 　His corpse when dead ; and madcap spring—
> (The virgin with the changeful eyes),
> 　Shall hear his loud artillery ring.

Among other favourable specimens of her handi-
craft, "Hannah Brown," "Lydia Lee," "Our
Village," "Home," and "Apple Gathering," may
be noted.

It is gratifying to be able to include in the
collection, two pieces in the Oxonian patois, the

first, I believe, ever attempted in that dialect.
These originally appeared in the columns of a
Banbury newspaper. "Mary and Me," and "Under
the Elms," are a couple of exquisite little domestic
idyls. Thus put before the public, there is no
saying what fruit they may bear. A dialect literature of modern growth, and of considerable
robustness, has sprung up in Lincolnshire, Cumberland, Lancashire, Yorkshire, Dorsetshire, and
many other English counties, much of which has
already taken deep root in the hearts of the
people.

Miss Smith died at 2 South Alfred-street, Carlisle,
on Wednesday, January 9th, 1889, in her sixty-
seventh year, and was interred in Carlisle cemetery,
where a plain stone marks her last resting place.
She left legacies to many relatives and friends, and
also to the Wesleyan Sunday School, Cropredy;
the Independent Sunday School, Great Bourton;
and the Unitarian Church, Carlisle.

Writing to an old and intimate friend shortly
before her death, and referring to her attendance at
the services of the Unitarians, Miss Smith said :—
"Should anything be said about me when I am

I. 20

gone, I wish you to explain that, although I attended the Unitarian Church in Carlisle for some time when I was able to go out, I never was a Unitarian. I do not believe in the Unitarian doctrine respecting the Atonement, and I went to the Church I speak of simply because I had reason to know that its members were being discourteously used by many persons on account of their theological opinions."

Speaking of this incident, her friend remarks :—"Well, fortunately it may be said, for herself, bowed down as she was with physical pain for which there was no remedy—the brave and pure-hearted woman who penned these words is now where, in all probability, neither the *odium theologicum* nor any other evil is known. For her also 'the day has dawned and the shadows have fled.' Her place from henceforth is with those among whom, throughout an endless existence, she will find nothing to regret—who know neither envy, malice, hatred, nor uncharitableness, but are as the angels of God."

APPENDIX.

---

*LETTERS FROM JANE WELSH AND
THOMAS CARLYLE.*

---

5 Cheyne Row, Chelsea,
16th January, 1854.

Dear Madam,

Your "faith in things unseen"—myself among them—
is very beautiful and affecting to me ; and likewise, I confess,
rather *infectious*. I cannot help believing in the good heart
and poetic nature, at least, of one who shows such belief in
my own "character," on evidence purely "internal."

And so, dear young lady, were I as influential as you
suppose me to be ; no more were needed, than what I gather
from your letter, to make me *use* my influence in your interest.
But indeed it were only deceiving you with false hopes to
promise myself at all likely to find you the situation you wish
for. There *is* no such situation, to the best of my knowledge,
as that of "Assistant to a Literary Lady." My position as
the wife of a *literary man* has thrown me much into the
society of *literary women*, that is to say of women who write
books as well as read them. But not one I know has an
assistant. Either these ladies follow literature as a trade—to

live by—in which case they could not pay an assistant; or following it for their pleasure, they want no assistant.

And, between ourselves, were such an assistantship created on purpose for you, you would find yourself—or I am greatly mistaken—no nearer, if so near, to "clear ideas" and "broad knowledge" than you are now—teaching a school.

It does sometimes—once in two or three years or so—happen to me that I can recommend a governess; and in case such opportunity present itself again, I will bear you in remembrance, at whatever distance of time. That is all I can promise, and I am sorry it is so little.

Meanwhile, believe a woman older than yourself, who has seen, and *seen thro'*, all you are now longing after. There is as little *nourishing* for an aspiring soul in literary society as in any civilized society one could name! And for "clear ideas" and "broad knowledge," they are not secreted in any corner of life, but lie in all life, for whoever has faculty to appreciate them.

Yours with all good wishes,
JANE WELSH CARLYLE.

Miss SMITH,
    11 West Tower-street, Carlisle.

---

5 CHEYNE ROW, CHELSEA,
11th January, 1857.

Dear Miss Smith,

    This time you come to me as an old acquaintance, whom I am glad to shake hands with again. The mere fact of your being still in the same position after so long an interval, and with such passionate inward protest as that first letter indicated, is a more authentic testimony to your worth, than if you had sent me a *certificate of character* signed by all the clergy and householders of Carlisle ! So many talents are wasted, so many enthusiasms turned to smoke, so many lives blighted, for want of a little patience and endurance ! for want of understanding and laying to heart that which you have so well expressed in these verses—the meaning of *the Present!* —for want of recognising, that it is not the greatness or littleness of "the duty nearest hand," but the spirit in which one does it, that makes one's doing noble or mean !

I can't think how people, who have any natural ambition, and any sense of power in them, escape going *mad* in a world like this, without the recognition of that ! I know I was very near *mad* when I found it out for myself (as one has to find out for one-self *everything* that is to be of any real practical use to one). Shall I tell you how it came into my head ? Perhaps it may be of comfort to you in similar moments of fatigue and disgust.

I had gone with my husband to live on a little estate of *peat bog*, that had descended to me, all the way down from John Welsh, the Covenanter, who married a daughter of John Knox. That didn't, I am ashamed to say, make me feel Craigenputtock a whit less of a peat bog, and most dreary, untoward place to live at ! In fact, it was sixteen miles distant on every side from all the conveniences of life—shops and even post office !

Further, we were very poor ; and further and worst, being an only child, and brought up to "great prospects," I was sublimely ignorant of every branch of useful knowledge, though a capital Latin scholar and a very fair mathematician !! It behoved me in these astonishing circumstances to learn— to *sew !* Husbands, I was shocked to find, wore their stockings into holes ! and were always losing buttons ! and *I* was expected to "look to all that !" Also, it behoved me to learn to *cook!* No *capable* servant choosing to live at "such an out of the way place," and my husband having "bad digestion," which complicated my difficulties dreadfully. The bread, above all, brought from Dumfries, "soured on his stomach," (Oh, Heavens !) and it was plainly my duty as a christian wife to bake at home !

So I sent for Cobbett's "Cottage Economy," and fell to work at a loaf of bread. But knowing nothing about the process of fermentation or the heat of ovens, it came to pass that my loaf got put into the oven at the time *myself* ought to have put into bed, and I remained the only person not asleep, in a house in the middle of a desert ! *One* o'clock struck, and then *two,* and then *three ;* and still I was sitting there in an intense solitude, my whole body aching with weariness, my heart aching with a sense of forlornness and degradation. "That I who had been so petted at home, whose comfort had been studied by everybody in the house, who had never been required to do anything but *cultivate my mind*, should have to pass all those hours of the night in watching *a loaf of bread!* which mightn't turn out bread after all !"

Such thoughts maddened me, till I laid down my head on the table, and sobbed aloud. It was then that somehow the idea of Benvenuto Cellini, sitting up all night watching his Pericles in the oven, came into my head ; and suddenly I asked myself, "After all ; in the sight of the upper powers, what is the mighty difference between a statue of Pericles and a loaf of bread, so that each be the thing one's hand hath found to do ? The man's determined will, his energy, his patience, his resource, were the really admirable things, of which the statue of Pericles was the mere chance expression.

If he had been a woman, living at Craigenputtock, with a dyspeptic husband, sixteen miles from a baker, and *he a bad one*—all these same qualities would have come out most fitly in a *good* loaf of bread !"

I cannot express what consolation this germ of an idea spread over my uncongenial life, during five years we lived at that savage place ; where my two immediate predecessors had gone *mad*, and the third had taken to drink !

But here am I beginning on a third little sheet [of note paper] and you are waiting for my opinion of the verses ! If you knew how completely I have lost all taste for poetry (so called), you would not have appealed to *my* judgment of all peoples ! Indeed, I should need to have been a poet born, to have continued writing or reading anything in verse, in the valley of the shadow of Mr. Carlyle's denunciations of verse ! I suppose, too, as one gets old, one naturally falls back on plain prose. But since you have asked my opinion, it would be discourteous to refuse it, even on the plea of incompetence.

I have read these verses very carefully several times over, and what I feel about them is that they are full of *thought* and *sense*, and deficient in *music*. They give me the impression of thought put into verse by *force of will*, rather than from a natural *taste for singing itself*.

My husband once asked Monkton Milnes why he put what he had to say into rhymes, "instead of JUST SAYING IT." The answer was—"Why you see, a very little thought goes so much further in verse !" Now, it seems to me, that *you* do not lie under that general exigence of modern poets, driving them on expedients to make a little thought go further than its natural length. There is more thought in the verses you have sent me, than might be elaborated into a long prose essay—more thought than in several volumes of poems, lying about on drawing room tables. But it is hurt rather than shown to advantage by the versification, which is hard and stiff—in a word, *unmusical.*

I should hardly have trusted my own judgment in such a matter, if Mr. Carlyle had not confirmed it. I read the verses to him, having first given him my notions about them, and he said—"Well, they are just what you said. The young lady has something in her to write, but she should resolve on sticking to prose." That from him was rather high praise, I assure you.

Yours truly,
JANE W. CARLYLE.

———

BAY HORSE, ALVERSTOKE, HANTS,
19th August, [1858.]

Dear Miss Smith,

"If this meet your eye," (as the *Times* advertisements say,) "you are requested to communicate" with Mrs. Carlyle, 5 Cheyne Row, Chelsea.

In fact, my present note is by way of *dove* sent forth from the ark, to try if it can find rest for the sole of its foot, and bring back an olive leaf from you to the effect that you are still in Carlisle, and still recollecting me with the old kind of feeling.

In that case, I should direct my energies towards "carrying out" an idea that has suggested itself to me of a meeting between us face to face.

I am going to Scotland, please God, the end of next week; and have arranged to sleep at Carlisle on the road. I cannot nor shall I be able to tell you beforehand what inn I shall stop at. I am in the hands of a lady who will meet me on my arrival, having come all the way from Nithsdale "to have my tea and bed ready." But if I were sure of your being still in Carlisle, and sure about your present address, I would find some means of letting you know my whereabouts and the hours of my stay.

I return to London on Monday next (23rd). If you get this note in regular course, please to send an answer to the old address. But besides the probability of your having changed your old address, I do not even remember quite certainly what it was!! So my dove goes forth "under difficulties"—decidedly.

Yours truly,
JANE WELSH CARLYLE.

Miss SMITH,
  9 (or 11) West Tower-street, Carlisle.

---

5 CHEYNE ROW.
(No date.)

Dear Miss Smith,

The pleasant surprise of your letter and book was enhanced for me by a coincidence really very curious! Only a few minutes before the postman left them, I had said to my husband as we sat at breakfast : "I wonder what Miss Smith is about? I have heard nothing from her since I saw her in Carlisle more than two years ago !"—And even while I spoke the postman had turned into our street with the letter and book! Was that *chance?* or *magnetism?* or *what?* Anyhow, it was something out of the jog-trot routine of one's life, and very acceptable! especially in this, "the gloomy month of November, when the people of England hang and drown themselves," [according to the French novelist !]

As for the *Dedication;* it could not but give me the warmest pleasure, that you should entertain such kind thoughts of me, and own to them before "the public ;" at the same time I underwent a little spasm of what we used to call, when children, *"thinking shame!"* I felt so little deserving of what you say there !

Dear Miss Smith ! I have no goodness "to speak of." In your intercourse with me, you have not seen me *tried.* Had you been a stupid, commonplace woman, there is every reason to believe you would have found me impatient, uncivil, sarcastic, anything and everything but *good.* As it was, I did but *gratify myself* in entering into correspondence with you—and whatever goodness you have seen in me has been goodness towards *myself.*

I have delayed writing from day to day in the wish to have "some reasonably good leisure"—that I might first read the book, and write a long letter. But my husband's friends, *"the Destinies,"* alias *"the Immortal Gods,"* have laid their heads together to overwhelm me with little worries, and with what Mr. C. calls "a pressure of things," till I hardly know what I am saying or doing.

You must excuse this scrubby note in the meantime, and perhaps another day, when you are in danger of forgetting me, the *long* letter will come into your hands.

Yours faithfully,
JANE WELSH CARLYLE.

CHEYNE ROW, CHELSEA,
10th April, [1865.]

Dear Miss Smith,

I am always glad to hear from you, and like to read your verses; tho' I often wish you had taken to writing practical *prose*, rather, that is, for *your own* sake. There is so little appreciation for poetry in these "hard times," and, alas! so little remuneration for it; while the appetite for magazine *Tales* and three-volume novels is getting to be a positive lupus —— ? something! I forget the full medical name of that disease which makes the victim gobble up, with unslaked voracity, pounds on pounds of raw beef and tallow candles! or anything that comes readiest.

I returned to London—by Carlisle again—about three months after I saw you, but I could not ask you to meet me at the station, even [if] it hadn't been too late at night. I felt too sick and nervous from the parting with my friends, and the long night journey before me, and the return in the morning to my poor old home, which I had been *carried* out of eight months before, with no particle of hope that I should ever set eyes on it again! I felt a sacred horror of the house in which I had suffered such tortures and such despair.

But so much had been done to change the aspect of my rooms, and I was received back with such enthusiasm, that all my morbid repugnance soon passed away, and *all* changes having a good effect on me, so even the change back to London had a beneficial effect on my health. I am still a very feeble, rather suffering creature, but so much better than I was a year ago, that I can never be thankful enough.

I am just returned from a month's stay in Devonshire, and it was there your letter reached me, when I was being driven thro' the loveliest country all days, and wearied to death at nights, so wrote not at all to anybody.

I wish you could have given me better news of yourself; and I wish most heartily that I could aid you in finding some position more suited to your needs and tastes. But my wishes are one thing, and my powers, alas! a quite other thing! At least be sure I will let slip no opportunity of serving you.

Believe me always truly yours,

JANE CARLYLE.

Miss SMITH,
　16 Finkle-street, Carlisle.

———

5 CHEYNE ROW, CHELSEA,
8 Decr., 1873.

Dear Madam,

I well enough remember the transient shadow of fine relation which you once had in this household; and in a mournful changed condition must always have; nor do you miscalculate the value I put upon it, or the feeling it awakens in me.

In looking over your book I am well pleased to find, what is rare in books, a perfect sincerity and worthiness of purpose; and I can easily believe that those clear utterances of your convictions and emotions about social and domestic matters may benefit many serious readers, now and in years coming. The question has sometimes arisen with me whether if you wrote down your ideas and feelings in simple and distinct prose, it might not be still better for your readers and yourself. This is a question I cannot pretend to decide; but my guess, if your circumstances suited and your inclinations prompted, would be clearly as above.

As to "Progress," about which there has been such chanting and trumpeting for the last half century, especially for the last score of years, I confess I could never see much in it, or decidedly discern any progress except in Smithwork and its adjuncts;—a very sooty, shrieky, and to me contemptible kind of progress,—yielding, as I often say, immensities of gold to those who least of all deserve it among us; and who can do, when one reflects upon it, nothing but mischief by being thus made kings among their fellows.

For the rest, I quite agree with you. All, or almost all the "Progress" in Smithwork and gold nuggets, is due to the Puritan ages; a fact which, on contrasting their moralities with our so miraculous smitheries, is a very melancholy one.

With many regards, yours sincerely,

T. CARLYLE.

Miss SMITH,
8 Finkle-street, Carlisle.

G. AND T. COWARD, PRINTERS, CARLISLE.

IN MEMORY OF

WILLIAM ROBERT PERCIVAL,

(HEREIN MENTIONED,)

A THOUGHTFUL AND CATHOLIC

MINDED MAN: A MAN OF MUCH

WISDOM.

www.ingramcontent.com/pod-product-compliance
Lightning Source LLC
Chambersburg PA
CBHW062036090426
42740CB00016B/2920